Advance Pr

From Gatekeeper to Trusted Advisor: Success Strategies for Today's HR Professional

"Kudos to Andria Corso who provides a practical model with tools, tips and techniques that will allow an HR leader from any size organization to become a true strategic business partner or an even stronger one. Using stories, examples and thought-provoking questions, **From Gatekeeper to Trusted Advisor** is an effective resource that demonstrates how to build credibility and link key HR objectives to top business objectives. Readers will learn how it is possible to not only get the coveted 'seat at the table', but a reserved one."

~ Suzanne Coonan, Vice President, Human Resources,
Lake Forest Graduate School of Management

"'How do we get a seat at the table?' That's been the proverbial $64M question for HR leaders for too many years. Fortunately, Andria Corso provides a practical, simple and actionable answer in **From Gatekeeper to Trusted Advisor** – you have to build a BRIDGE. With a clear approach based on deep experience, Corso uses her Bridge Model to help HR leaders identify not just what to do but how to do it to get that seat."

~ Scott Eblin, President of The Eblin Group and author of
The Next Level: What Insiders Know About Executive Success

"**From Gatekeeper to Trusted Advisor** is a much-needed, easy to read guide for anyone who wants to be a valued and respected HR leader. It shows the vital behaviors and practices required of HR to be courageous, strong and valued partners and leaders in their businesses today."

~ Bruce Tulgan, author of *It's Okay to Be the Boss*,
Founder and chairman of RainmakerThinking, Inc.

"The most practical and powerful book I have seen for HR professionals. Corso shares a candid and accurate assessment of where the HR profession is headed in the real business world. A must read for HR professionals willing to ask the question needing to be asked: How do we truly add value? Corso delivers a simple yet powerful approach to drive results."

~ Jacqueline Chaffee, Senior Director, Learning & Talent Management, CHR US/Americas Siemens Corporation

"Andria Corso has got it right. This book is hard hitting – with straight talk about practical and proven ways to transform HR professionals from second class to first class citizens at all levels within their organizations. Andria is a seasoned veteran who combines her own experience with lessons gleaned from senior leaders to produce powerful prescriptions that can be mapped to the real world of the HR professional. The book will serve first as a primer to HR professionals interested in developing themselves and seeking ways to improve their competency. It will also serve as a refresher to those already operating at a high level of capabilities and influence. Finally, senior executives and managers should have this book as a desk reference to aid in their efforts to facilitate their HR leaders to move **From Gatekeeper to Trusted Advisor.**"

~ Bill Ewald, PhD., Senior Fellow, ICF International

"There's a lot to learn in Andria Corso's **From Gatekeeper to Trusted Advisor.** It's a helpful mix of authentic real-world examples, practical advice, information, checklists, and probing questions. This book should be required reading for all HR professionals - or at least those who are concerned about the skills and competencies necessary to do a good job!"

~ Sharon Armstrong, Author of *The Essential Performance Review Handbook, The Essential HR Handbook,* and *Stress-free Performance Appraisals*

"In, **From Gate Keeper to Trusted Advisor,** Ms. Corso presents a value-added approach that HR professionals should look to adopt. The model she defines promotes a continuous exchange of information between HR and key stakeholders. That positions HR executives to be trusted advisors because they know how to be proactively involved in helping their clients understand, and prepare for, the future challenges that their businesses will face."

~ Kendrew H. Colton, Partner, Fitch, Even, Tabin, & Flannery

"While Andria's advice to "speak the client's language" should be evident to all HR professionals, I can recall my own failures that can be directly attributed to not following this basic principle. Her examples remind all of us that influencing leaders is about demonstrating our value to them, not about "teaching them" what they need to know about HR."

~ Cynthia A. Karst, Senior Principal Consultant, RGS

"I wish every HR professional would read Ms. Corso's book and pay close attention to her council to know your clients' business and reflect that knowledge in your HR priorities. HR executives who work successfully with me know my top 3 priorities because they took the time to ask me to define them. That truly makes them my trusted advisors because they understand how to help me craft solutions that meet my challenges."

~Ramesh Thadani, Vice President, International Operations, Graduate Management Admissions Council

"Andria Corso's "rule of focus" could be renamed the "golden rule of defining value." Ms. Corso's explanation of the need to gain and maintain stakeholder engagement throughout the lifecycle of an HR initiative is foundational to any effort that ultimately gains traction, executive sponsorship, and funding."

- Rick Wallace, Vice President, Learning & Development for North America, Schneider Electric

Kim—
All my best,
Andrea Corso

ANDRIA L. CORSO

FROM GATEKEEPER
to TRUSTED ADVISOR

SUCCESS STRATEGIES FOR
TODAY'S HR PROFESSIONAL

Love Your Life
LOVE YOUR LIFE PUBLISHING, INC.

From Gatekeeper to Trusted Advisor: Success Strategies for Today's HR Professional ©2010 by Andria L. Corso

All rights reserved. No part of this book may be used or reproduced in any manner whatsoever without written permission except in the case of brief quotations embodied in articles and reviews.

Love Your Life

Love Your Life Publishing, Inc.
7127 Mexico Road Suite 121
Saint Peters, MO 63376
www.LoveYourLifePublishing.com
publisher@LoveYourLifePublishing.com

ISBN: 978-1-934509-33-3
Library of Congress Control Number: 2010936607

Printed in the United States of America

Cover and Internal Design by: www.Cyanotype.ca
Editing by: Gwen Hoffnagle
First Printing: 2010

This book is dedicated to my HR colleagues.

In the words of Mahatma Gandhi,
"Be the change you wish to see in the world."

ACKNOWLEDGEMENTS

I have always loved to write (and thankfully still do), and although I had heard that writing a book is a huge task, I did not realize how huge it truly was until now. As with any large undertaking in life, I could not have done it without the support of many people who I am lucky to have in my life.

To my Mom: for your endless support of my pursuing my dreams and your continuous encouragement and prayers. I am so blessed to have you.

To my Dad: for planting the seed for me to write this book (which started the wheels in motion), and for always making me believe I could do anything I wanted.

To Debra: for your endless belief in me and for teaching me to always follow my heart and go with my gut.

To Matt: for your never-ending confidence in me, your love and unconditional support, and for showing me what it truly means to live my life on purpose.

To Smith: my very best friend. Thank you for talking me through the past twenty-something years.

To all the people I interviewed for the book: your insights and input made this book what it is. I am truly grateful that you donated your time and wisdom to this book, my readers and me.

To all of my family, friends and colleagues who supported me and encouraged me throughout this process (too many of you to list!): I appreciate your constant support and thoughts of encouragement.

To the wonderful team at Love Your Life Publishing: what a blessing it has been to have had all your guidance, starting with the Get Your Book Done program through the entire publication process. I have learned so much! Thank you for your patience and kindness!

And finally, a big thanks to my basset hounds, Daisy and Swanny: for lying at my feet for countless hours while I wrote. You made that time so very peaceful.

TABLE OF CONTENTS

INTRODUCTION: WHY WE ARE HERE TODAY

The following conversation occurred between an HR director and two of the business leaders she supports:

HR Director: I received the email you sent with your questions about whether to relocate your employee or just put him on extended travel.

Leader #1: Oh, good, I really was hoping we could accommodate the travel versus having to relocate the employee.

Leader #2: I think we've done something like this before with other employees in the same situation.

HR Director: I actually think we should engage the finance department to determine how much the travel will cost and then make a decision based on that. I can get the staffing manager involved for more information on the relocation package specifics, but I don't think we need to go to him just yet.

Leader #1: Oh, great! I'd rather not go to HR at all.

Leader #2: Yes, I absolutely agree with that! (laugh)

HR Director: But I am HR…

(Leader #1 and #2 laugh.)

Leader #1: Oh, Jane, we really don't think of you as being part of them. We don't really consider you "HR".

(The HR director is silent… a bit confused.)

Leader #2: Trust me, that is a GOOD thing.

Some of you reading this might think that conversation went great. Business leaders were consulting with a human resources professional and not thinking of her as part of the human resources department. Maybe there are aspects of that which are positive, yet this conversation implied that it was better to not be associated with HR. The HR person involved in this discussion was actually proud of being part of the human resources department, yet what the leaders conveyed was that being part of the HR department is not where you want to be nor does it earn you respect or credibility; that it is better to not be considered part of that department.

I wrote *From Gatekeeper to Trusted Advisor: Success Strategies for Today's HR Professional* for HR professionals. I wrote it to help them manage the perception that many business leaders have that it is better to be disassociated from the HR function. This book takes readers on a journey of experiences from inside Fortune 500 companies, as well as small and mid-size companies, with senior HR leaders who have had a seat at the table with executives and know what it takes to be seen as a valued asset and a trusted advisor to senior leadership and C-suite teams. It is based on countless examples and perspectives from over 100 senior HR and business leaders with whom I interacted and interviewed, and my own fifteen-year experience with Fortune 500 companies. I am sharing these experiences and information in an effort to help change the perception of the human resources function, one person at a time.

How far has the HR function evolved over the years? Have we, as HR professionals, broken through the barriers of the old administrative-type roles? Do we have a seat at the table with our business leaders, and is it a respected seat for us? If you ask HR professionals these questions, they will all agree that HR has greatly evolved over the years. HR professionals have gone from being focused on administrative tasks such as payroll and benefits, to being strategic business partners for their organizations.

HR professionals, for the most part, have a strong desire to add value to their organization and align their work with that which most benefits their business and has direct impact on business results. Yet business leaders do not have the same feelings about the HR function as HR professionals have about themselves. True, many company leaders respect HR professionals and expect them to be a part of making key business decisions; yet when asking leaders to articulate the true value that the HR department adds, most make comments such as, *"They keep us out of trouble," "They staff my programs,"* or *"They remind me what I cannot do."*

HR professionals want to be hearing different things. In his book, *Winning,* Jack Welch said, "To manage people well, companies should elevate HR to a position of power and primacy in the organization and make sure HR people have the special qualities to help managers build leaders and careers." HR professionals want to be in a respected place of power and primacy.

Those "special qualities" that Jack Welch refers to are those competencies that experts such as Richard Beatty, Mark Huselid and Dave Ulrich have spent years defining for the human resource profession. HR professionals need to possess certain skills and competencies to be able to do their jobs. Throughout the past twenty years, a great deal of research has been conducted and shared with HR professionals about what capabilities are required for them to adequately perform their roles. These include being credible activists, culture and change stewards, talent managers, organization designers, strategy architects, operational executors and business allies (Ulrich et al, 2008, *HR Competencies*). Most business leaders and HR professionals would agree that HR professionals could learn any of these competencies that they do not already possess. Yet the question still remains: Why are HR professionals still seen as gatekeepers, or often referred to as "The Business Prevention Department"? What is still missing? If HR professionals have (or can learn) the competencies, is the missing piece that they are not practicing the skills effectively and acting in ways to best showcase these competencies?

In 2007, there was an article published in *Fast Company* magazine titled, "Why We Hate HR". The article highlighted numerous reasons why the human resources department is hated. These included: HR professionals' lack of knowledge and interest in their company's core customers; their desire to work in ways that are efficient and consistent as opposed to those that add value; their unwillingness to be flexible, step out of the "rules" box, or make exceptions for the sake of adding value to the organization; and their desire to forfeit long-term value for short-term efficiency. The article stated that the human resources profession is stuck in the past and unable to propel itself forward. The article closed with a great point about how HR is the only department in the organization that has the ability to discover things about the business through the eyes of its people and its talent, and though this should give companies a huge competitive advantage, in most organizations this opportunity is wasted.

Why is this opportunity wasted? Because, as a group, HR professionals are still not respected enough for business leaders to save them a seat at the decision-making table. We are still not in a position to consistently share what we are discovering about the business through its people and talent. We are the group that leaders should not be starting a meeting without, yet are likely to be the group whom they most desire to not have attend their meetings. HR professionals want and deserve to be trusted advisors, yet we are still perceived as gatekeepers and roadblocks.

The *UK Times* published an online article in 2008 that addressed the fact that companies have reduced their HR staffs by nearly 30% in recent years (as reported by Deloitte), and that leaders are embracing the demise of the HR function. The main reason why leaders embrace this demise is because they feel that the HR department is inflexible. Their perception is that HR policies are written for a small percentage of employees who are unproductive and "bad" as opposed to being written for the majority of the workforce; hence the policies are restrictive and tend to tie leaders' hands. This adds to the perception that HR, as a profession, is comprised of individuals who are inflexible and unwilling to make exceptions, as well as being road-blockers and gatekeepers.

What does this all mean for the HR profession? Clearly the perception needs to change, and the only ones who can change that perception are individual HR folks, one person at a time. I wrote *From Gatekeeper to Trusted Advisor: Success Strategies for Today's HR Professional* to help HR professionals begin to change the way they are viewed by the business leaders and employees they support. I want to help us lose these nagging negative titles and be the trusted advisors we deserve to be and that our companies need. The book primarily focuses on the attitudes, behaviors and practices required to be trusted advisors in the high-stakes and highly-intense corporate world. HR professionals know (and most are quite skilled in) the competencies required of them in order to effectively support business objectives; however, the competencies are only one part of the equation. Behaviors and actual practices are the other parts of the equation and are the focal points of this book.

How do HR professionals behave in order to build trust and establish credibility so they can implement the countless HR programs that are required? What actions must they take to build trust and credibility and have a seat at the decision-making table?

If the perception does not change, the human resources profession is in danger of completely losing its credibility and eventually becoming defunct. Some large corporations have begun to fill HR jobs with employees who are not HR professionals. Recently, in a Fortune 100 company, Jennifer, the corporate director of talent management, transferred to a new assignment. Ryan, the senior vice president of HR, was considering replacing Jennifer with a high potential business leader from inside the corporation. This was someone with no HR experience, yet he was being considered for a critical HR position. Jennifer was not happy about the direction that her senior leadership was headed because she was an HR professional with over ten years of experience and an advanced degree in human resources. Those credentials added to her success in the role of corporate director of talent management. Why put an individual with an engineering degree (for example) in charge of talent management for a 100,000-employee organization? Would you put an HR person in charge of the software development department in the same organization? The answer to that question is no. Yet even Ryan, the senior vice president of HR, had the perception that someone could handle this type of work without any HR background or education, that the required HR skills could be learned, and that anyone smart enough could fill the position and learn the necessary skills to be successful. Theory has it that Ryan's perception was really not his own but that of the senior executive staff, and that he acquiesced to them in considering a non-HR person for a critical HR role.

Such sentiments are not the truth of HR professionals. They know that they are the right people to fill these jobs and they need to change current perceptions about their profession or risk becoming obsolete. In the example above, Jennifer's role was eventually filled by an HR professional with many years of experience as well as advanced education in HR. Yet the fact that there was even consideration about filling that job with someone outside of HR is unnerving to those in the HR field.

Another example of such perceptions is one from a Fortune 500 company. The senior vice president of HR was retiring and the rumor was that there was not a viable HR successor internal to the company. The CEO was not of the mindset to hire someone who would be reporting directly to him from outside of the company. Speculation began within the company that the role would be filled by someone internal but outside of the human resources department. In fact, a few senior leaders in the organization began vying for the position and even spoke to the CEO and the incumbent senior vice president of HR about their belief that they could take on the role and create a huge positive impact.

Yet another example occurred recently in a school district in Connecticut in which the director of technology was appointed as the superintendent for human resources. This was the second time in three years that the school district superintendent recommended a director of technology to lead the HR department. The superintendent indicated that he looked for a highly-talented individual who could rapidly learn the details of the job as opposed to a highly-talented human resources leader who already had the necessary technical knowledge and a familiarity with the broad scope of responsibilities for the job.

Again, the question comes up: Is it logical to ask an HR professional to become the vice president of engineering? Probably not. Yet there is a belief, by some, that HR roles can be successfully handled by anyone who has been a successful leader.

HR professionals are at a critical crossroads. We must retain our right to the positions for which we have been educated and groomed. We must work hard to change the perception of HR professionals as gatekeepers who are not interested in the needs of the business but only in consistency, efficiency and enforcing rules.

It should be noted that perceptions about HR professionals vary according to the level of the leader. In many organizations, executive and senior-level leaders are profound supporters of HR and have a good understanding of the need for HR programs and what HR professionals are trying to achieve through their work. Such leaders tend to be seasoned individuals who understand why HR programs can take a long time to implement and why specific HR policies are required. "Corporate responsibility" is better understood at the top. This perception diminishes the lower the level of the leader, as they are less informed about the strategic need for, and the role of, an HR partner. Since there are far fewer senior and executive leaders in organizations, it is really the majority of leaders who perceive HR as being encumbered by rules and processes and having little value to add to the organization. This perception needs to change.

Could it be that HR continues to grapple with an inherent paradox? HR professionals clearly want to increase their value and be seen as strategic resources. Yet the hard truth is that this is often why we create complex processes and programs and over-engineer our work. We believe this makes us indispensible, when, in reality, it makes us infuriating. Because we often make simple things seem complex, we end up with titles like "Human Restraint Department", and the leaders we support often would rather proceed without us. The result of such efforts is that the HR department loses credibility and is devalued, when all we were trying to do was prove our value. The consequences of not addressing this are that HR professionals lose those top HR positions to operational or functional business leaders, and the profession as a whole continues to lose credibility and becomes more and more outsourced.

HR professionals make a habit of getting in their own way. And why is that? Do we have the wrong attitude about our role? Another hard truth is that yes, we probably do. We often feel the pressure of conforming to organizational constraints and continue to tell the old story that our job is to be a taskmaster, a cop, a gatekeeper, and to keep everyone out of trouble. These attitudes get in the way of becoming trusted advisors. This book explores these attitudes and provides solutions for changing them.

I interviewed an HR vice president for a Fortune 500 information technology company who did not "grow up" in the field of HR. She has a very different perspective from most HR professionals regarding who is leading the HR function. She believes that the most dramatic and effective way to address this perception issue is to put people who are not from HR in the top HR jobs. She feels that this will change perceptions and shift the current mindset, and that companies that place non-HR professionals in top HR positions will become "Academy HR" role models for other companies. This individual has done many wonderful things to try to shift the perception of HR inside and outside of her large organization, yet her viewpoint is not one that the HR profession would want to promote. It is my perspective, and the perspective of many interviewed for this book, that putting non-HR people in top-level HR jobs is not the right path to take to change the perception. I believe HR professionals should show that they are committed to changing the perception by taking the necessary steps to change their own behaviors and practices.

The next twelve chapters will go inside some of the world's largest corporations, as well as many well-known mid-sized and smaller companies, where HR professionals have learned through years of trial and error what it takes to be seen as valued assets and trusted advisors to their senior leadership teams. The book is divided into six sections and includes checklists, templates, tip sheets and exercises for HR professionals to use and apply in their daily work lives. The book sections align to the six principles of what I have labeled the Bridge Model. The model comprises the attitudes, behaviors and practices required of HR professionals to shift from being gatekeepers to trusted advisors. These principles can help you become the "bridge" for your organization's success as opposed to being a roadblock. The Bridge Principles are:

I. **Build Your Base**

II. **Respond Responsibly**

III. **Influence Impeccably**

IV. **Distinguish Yourself**

V. **Get Out of The Way**

VI. **Encourage Expectation**

Each Bridge Principle contains two concepts and practical applications for utilizing the principle in your own situations. In addition, each principle includes a case study or a practical, real world example based on that specific concept. The case studies and examples come from many interviews that I conducted with well-respected senior HR and business leaders across various industries about the specific behaviors that equate to "trusted advisor", as well as from my own experiences at Fortune 500 companies. It should be noted that in order to protect the confidentiality of the individuals interviewed and their companies, their names have been changed. Although the examples and stories are real-life, the names are not.

The book is designed so readers can easily follow the Bridge Principles and have useful, practical and applicable tools and examples to walk away with and implement in their day-to-day lives. (Each template, tip sheet or exercise contained in the book is available to readers as a free download at: www.trustedadvisorreaderspage.com).

Through application of these principles, readers become the bridge to their organization's success. They can rid themselves of titles such as "Human Restraint Department", and become trusted HR advisors without whom leaders will not start a meeting.

---— PRINCIPLE I ——---

BUILD YOUR BASE

A base, or a foundation, sets a structure in place. If the base is not solid, the structure can be unstable. Building a foundation sets the climate for how that specific item will hold up and live out its existence. It is not very easy to rebuild a faulty foundation, especially after the structure on top is completed. The same holds true for relationships. If the base is not solid, the way in which that relationship evolves will likely be unstable. This is why building a solid base – your solid base – with clients is the first crucial principle of the Bridge Model.

Note: When the term "clients" is used in this book, it means everyone in your company – your internal clients. These are the employees and leaders with whom you work and support as an HR professional. Everyone who may be influenced by your actions as an HR professional should be treated with great customer service - like a client. And when the term "leaders" is used, it means a particular subset of your clients. Clients comprise all employees and stakeholders, including those in leadership roles, but many examples cited in the book refer specifically to those clients in leadership roles. In those instances, the term "leaders" is used.

CHAPTER 1

ATTITUDES AND AUTHENTICITY

DICTIONARY.COM DEFINES "TRUST" AS "RELIANCE ON the integrity, strength, ability, and surety of a person or thing; confidence." "Advisor" is defined as "someone who gives counsel to; offers an opinion or suggestion; who consults with others." Putting those two definitions together gives us the definition of a trusted advisor: one who has the integrity, strength, ability and confidence to give counsel; one who is relied upon to consult or offer an opinion. This is the definition to reference throughout this book as you discover how to become a trusted advisor. This is the "end state" for HR professionals: to be trusted advisors to their clients.

The first step to reach that state is to build the foundation of the relationship. Build a foundation that will allow you, the HR advisor, to be seen as the confident, trustworthy giver of advice and counsel. When you think about building foundations and relationships, you need to have the right attitudes about those relationships to build them solidly. Attitudes are usually positive or negative, good or bad, and are fueled with energy.

Everyone has had experiences in which someone walks into the room and their entire demeanor and stance exudes a bad or negative attitude; you can feel the tension and negative vibrations when they walk into the room. You can also sense when someone walks into a room with a positive vibration and energy that make those in the room feel good, light and full of life. You know how you react to the person with the negative attitude versus the person with the positive attitude. Most people want to avoid the person with the negative attitude and embrace the person with the positive attitude. Clearly, one would prefer to be around someone who is full of life and good energy.

What kind of energy do you bring into a room? A senior leader in a large consulting company recently stated, "HR is the only group that can light up a room by leaving it." That statement definitely speaks to the type of energy that some HR professionals bring into a room.

Attitudes are typically formed based on our history and experiences with events and people. Individuals might form a negative attitude about going to the doctor's office because history tells them that the doctor will be running an hour behind schedule and they will waste an hour sitting in the waiting room. They might form a positive attitude about going to watch a concert by a well-known band because history tells them that this will be a fun and exciting experience. Yet attitudes are also choices. Individuals get to choose what type of attitude they will take with them to each encounter. No matter where you are going or what you are doing, you get the choice of taking either a negative attitude or a positive attitude along. You could choose to feel more positive about going to the doctor's office by regarding the extra waiting time as an opportunity to catch up on reading or to just sit and do nothing for a change. And you could choose to feel negative about going to the concert because of all the traffic, crowds and long lines. It is all a matter of how you view it.

What attitudes are you taking into your professional life each day? Are you feeling optimistic about your ability to work with and partner with others and to encourage the best from yourself and your clients? Or are you feeling unenthusiastic and off-putting about your ability to collaborate and partner with your clients?

Building a base or foundational relationship of any kind begins by taking a look inside yourself and what attitudes you are harboring. In order to be an effective and trusted HR advisor, you should first check your attitude. Check to see if it is good or bad. Check to see if you are choosing your attitude or letting past events and circumstances dictate it. If it happens to be a day when you feel an unconstructive and pessimistic attitude prevailing, then check those feelings at the door of your office building and leave them there until you go home later in the day. You can pick them up on your way out if you still feel like dragging them home with you.

If you are to be a trusted advisor, you should be committed to showing up every day with the best possible attitude, one that enables you to confidently give counsel, consult and collaborate. You get to choose whether or not you want to do this and if you choose to do this more frequently than not, you are well on your way to trusted advisor status. If you choose a negative or disapproving attitude the majority of the time, you will likely be thought of as a gatekeeper. You can choose to be the HR advisor who actually lights up the room when you walk in, or to light it up by leaving.

Attitudes are actually hypothetical constructs that represent our degree of like or dislike about a topic or situation, and they can change as a result of experience or expectation. As was stated earlier using the example of the doctor's office and the concert, if you expect something to be a positive experience, you will likely have a more affirmative attitude about it, whereas if you expect something to be unpleasant, you are likely to have a negative attitude about it.

Attitudes influence behaviors. Behaviors are actions or reactions to people, objects or situations, and are the manner in which we conduct ourselves. People behave not only as a reaction to what is going on around them but also as the result of their attitude. Behaviors that equate to being a trusted advisor include things like being collaborative, influential, open, responsive, confident, self-assured, straightforward, honest, and authentic. These are only a few of the many behaviors that will be reviewed in much greater detail later in this book. The attitudes that HR professionals need to behave as trusted advisors are positive, encouraging, affirmative and optimistic.

Oftentimes HR professionals have attitudes that prevent or constrain them from being trusted advisors. Their own self-image reflects a tradition of upholding the laws, policies and rules that govern organizational employment practices. This is the group that ensures everyone stays out of trouble. That sounds like the job of a law enforcement officer, not that of a strategic and trusted HR professional. Yes, human resources professionals do have the responsibility to ensure that business leaders adhere to certain employment laws and regulations, but their role is to provide advice and counsel on how to act and perform within the specific guidelines of these regulations. Their role is not to be the police officer. The attitude of one who provides guidelines and advice is a positive attitude that promotes collaborative behaviors. The attitude of one who is in the role of a police officer is a severe and strict attitude that tends to instill anxiety and promote apprehensive and fearful behaviors. Remember that you have the choice of the attitude you take with you each day. Make the choice that will enable you to be a trusted advisor.

This brings us to the next topic about attitudes and the behaviors that they drive, and that is authenticity. Authenticity is the quality of being genuine and trustworthy. An online dictionary says that it is "undisputed credibility." As trusted advisors, HR professionals should demonstrate authenticity. If you are not believable, your clients will pick up on that immediately. As you think about checking your attitude and understanding what is required of you to be a partner to your organizational leaders, think also about your authenticity. Do you truly want to be the person who acts as a bridge or are you frustrated by the thought of collaborating with organizational leaders? You should answer this question honestly. If your answer is that collaboration is frustrating and you would rather not have to deal with the types of situations that require teaming up, working in partnership, and finding solutions, then you are probably in the wrong profession.

HR professionals have been quoted as saying, "I am a people person" to the tune of it becoming a cliché and almost laughable. However, there is a lot to be said about that comment. Trusted advisors from any background need to genuinely and authentically want to help and assist others to reach their best. They should desire the best possible outcome for their clients and offer up their time, energy and resources in assisting them with their objectives.

One can clearly see when someone is being authentic and truly desires to partner and collaborate with others. That person is open and receptive to ideas and energizes others through their collaboration. They are able to bring people together in a way that generates solutions and creates consensus. That sounds quite idealistic, and perhaps is not attainable 100% of the time; however, if you are truly in the mindset of partnering and have a positive attitude about being a bridge to your clients' success, then you are generating that consensus and energy the majority of the time, because you are doing it with an attitude of genuinely trying to help. True and trusted HR advisors are those who are as excited on day one of the new assignment as they are on day 1,000. Perhaps the excitement is for different reasons on day 1,000, but they are eager to participate and partner with their clients for success no matter how long they have been in the role.

A great example of an attitude like this came from a senior HR leader, Paul, who works for a large information technology company. Paul was viewed as a highly-credible and trusted HR advisor by the senior leaders in his company. He put forth a "customer-driven" attitude when dealing with his colleagues and clients. He had a variety of HR and business positions within his organization, which added to his credibility. Yet he was also focused on putting his clients' needs first (think: "the customer comes first") and was committed to understanding their issues in a collaborative manner to come up with solutions that worked. Paul focused on having a deep understanding of the business issues at hand and how HR initiatives impact these issues. This enabled him to provide solid, high-quality advice and suggestions in support of his clients' reaching their desired outcomes. Paul made it a priority to understand his clients and their goals. He gained knowledge about circumstances in which current HR processes hinder speed so that he could work with his clients to come up with the most efficient ways to execute plans and programs within specified guidelines and policies. He truly had a customer-driven orientation towards his clients and demonstrated it repeatedly in the variety of positions he held within the company.

Paul also had a very positive attitude toward learning and expanding his knowledge, not only in regard to his clients' particular business areas, but also about the company as a whole. By exposing himself to a variety of different businesses and assignments within the larger corporation, he was able to demonstrate that he had the type of credibility that deserved trusted advisor status. He is a great example of keeping one's attitude open to new experiences and learning, and, most importantly, to being focused on treating clients with a customer-driven orientation.

If you honestly do not want to be a collaborative partner or to be customer-oriented, then you create resistance. Despite how much you may want to pretend, the energy and vibes you give off will tell a different story. Your clients will likely see through this, and it can often be the start of negative perceptions about HR. You have to build relationships and be collaborative to be a trusted HR advisor. If you can't do that, close this book and find yourself another profession in which you do not have to interact or partner with other people. Don't pretend that you want to be doing something that is not in keeping with who you are as a person. It's okay – not everyone is meant to be an HR partner and not everyone is able to be a trusted advisor. This is not about having a bad day or feeling the occasional negative attitude that needs to be adjusted. This is about determining whether or not you can be a genuine trusted advisor and whether or not you have that desire inside of you to affect the attitudes and behaviors required to do so.

What are your values? Stop and think about this for a moment. Do you value being with others or being alone? What are your top five values? Are you living a life that is in line with those values? To be even more straightforward, you either have it or you do not. Debra, a trusted HR advisor who leads the talent development department for a Fortune 500 information technology company, expressed that those HR people who "have it" are confident enough to know that they truly desire to partner with their clients and act as servers of the business. This does not mean that they are *servants*, but are those who serve the business with the courage of their convictions and with the pride of knowing who they are and what they bring to the table.

Answering these questions about your values and being true to yourself is the only way to live a fulfilled life; answering these questions and being true to yourself is the only way that you will ever be able to do what you are truly meant to do. Hopefully, if you are still reading this, it is because you sincerely want to be a trusted advisor. If not, be true to yourself and your clients and do something that you are truly meant to do.

Once you determine that you are being true to yourself and are coming from a place of authenticity, it is time to determine what being authentic, within reason, means. "Authentic within reason" means that you are a genuine HR partner to your clients. It means that you are striving to be the trusted advisor and you are doing it in a top-notch, professional manner. Often people take their desire to be authentic and genuine to an extreme so that it becomes a derailer to success, as opposed to an enabler of success. For example, an HR leader who was working to enable his team to be more authentic ended up having to deal with a performance issue. There was a person on his team whose efforts to be true to himself resulted in his making comments that were perceived by others as demeaning. This individual had always been a very direct, "tell it like it is" person and he ended up, inadvertently, hurting others' feelings.

This takes us back to what it means to be "authentic within reason". You most certainly want to be true to yourself in your actions and in how you spend your time. However, you should also remain acutely aware of how your behaviors and actions impact those around you. Trusted advisors do not isolate others but instead work to bring them together. They genuinely desire the best for everyone. They will tell it like it is, but they do so from a place of wanting the best for everyone involved. This is being authentic within reason; this is filtering your genuine thoughts for the benefit of the greater group; this is censored authenticity as opposed to uncensored authenticity, and this is how trusted HR advisors are true to themselves and their clients.

Being authentic with yourself and your clients enables you to act in a way that supports them and reveals your desire to partner with them. One of the key ways to start the partnership and begin building the base is to truly understand their mission, vision and strategy. This is typically your client's foundation. It is what they build their business upon and the basis for their actions and behaviors. As a trusted HR advisor, it is your responsibility to develop the relationship with that vision foremost in your mind. If you are able to do this, you can establish a strong, solid foundation that you and your client share as the root of your relationship. You can then hold this vision for your clients as you support them in your trusted advisor role.

In order to be able to do all this, you first have to reach out and understand the mission, vision and strategy. This will be covered in greater detail in Chapter 2, Begin with the End in Mind. However, it is important to touch upon it here because it speaks to being authentic and ensuring that your client is also being true to the vision. It also speaks to having the right attitudes that support this very important behavior of holding the client's vision for them.

For example, Nicole, an HR leader, was working with her client on a difficult affordability and cost-cutting challenge that would potentially impact headcount and possibly cause a reduction in force. This particular division of the company focused on information technology security. Their mission and vision was to safeguard and enhance the information technology infrastructure and processes and to simplify the way in which the processes were executed. When developing the strategy to support this mission and vision, the "simplify" piece equated to compressing procedures and combining cumbersome multiple and repetitive systems. Nicole worked closely with this leadership team and was actively engaged in developing a strategy to support the vision, so she knew it very well. However, when there was a cost-cutting challenge presented to the vice president of this group, he immediately decided that a workforce reduction was the answer to the affordability issues. He felt that this would not only meet the financial needs of the business but would also support the vision through simplification. Because Nicole had worked closely with this client throughout the mission, vision and strategy development, she knew that simplifying did not necessarily mean cutting heads. In fact, she knew that the true meaning of simplification related to reduction in systems and procedures and not necessarily heads.

Of course, oftentimes the reduction of systems and procedures results in headcount reduction, but the initial and immediate response from her client was purely one of "reduce heads." As a trusted advisor, Nicole knew that it was her responsibility to ensure that her client was being authentic himself and furthering the vision of his division. She was displaying the positive attitude of wanting the best for her client, and acted accordingly. She calmly approached him with a mindset of wanting to assist him in coming up with a solution to a difficult problem that was impacting his business. Her entire demeanor was one that exuded these feelings so he was very open to her thoughts and ideas. She suggested that the headcount reduction was not the first step to take. She proposed that they take the steps to reduce some of the cumbersome processes and repetitive systems first, and then see if headcount reductions were still necessary. The quick solution would have been to select a percentage of the total headcount that would meet the financial challenges that the business was facing. The solution that Nicole presented to her client was longer and more involved, yet it was the right thing to do and was ultimately their final solution.

This is an example of how, by using the right attitudes and behaviors, an HR professional was able to act as a trusted advisor to her client and exert appropriate influence. Because she had an authentic desire to help find the best solution, her client listened to her and heeded her advice. Had Nicole come from a disingenuous place with a poor attitude, the outcome could have been (and likely would have been) quite different. Having the right attitudes and being authentic is the first vital step to take to be able to build your base for being a trusted advisor; doing this will ease you into the rest of the journey.

"There can be no happiness if the things we believe in are different from the things we do."
~ FREYA MADELINE STARK

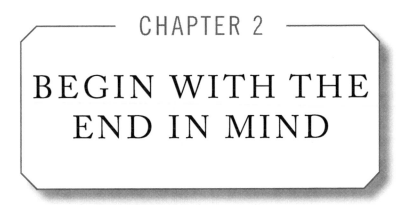

CHAPTER 2

BEGIN WITH THE END IN MIND

*"If you do not know where you are going,
you'll end up someplace else"*

— YOGI BERRA

YOU NOW KNOW YOU HAVE THE RIGHT ATTITUDE TO be a trusted advisor, and you should take the steps to keep that attitude in the forefront of your mind and heart and behave in ways that promote that attitude. How can you effectively do this? By beginning with the end in mind. Start from the end point. What does your ideal relationship with those you work with and support look like? Can you see it in your mind? Can you feel how it clicks and connects people together? Are you visualizing something that is full of honesty, candor, trust and partnership? Keep that image in your mind as you begin to build your relationships with the leaders and employees you support.

Beginning with the end mind is essential in building relationships with your clients. Successfully developing and maintaining strong relationships involves actions that HR professionals should take as well as actions that business leaders should take. As an HR professional, a starting point in reaching the desired end state is to take the initiative to have one-on-one meetings with the key stakeholders and leaders in the organizations you support. Schedule meetings (face-to-face whenever possible) to discover their key business issues and objectives and determine how HR can best support them in reaching these objectives.

This is a common practice of Dave, a seasoned HR vice president at a Fortune 100 retail company who worked his way up through the ranks of his company. Dave is well known for his candor and integrity as well as the high level of credibility he has with the business leaders he has supported throughout his twenty-year career. Dave takes sufficient time in a new assignment to get to know all the business leaders he is supporting and gains a solid understanding of their particular business issues as well as their objectives. He also solicits their input about how HR can provide the best support and he gets full disclosure about what has worked for them with HR in the past and what has not worked. This gives him a great starting point.

In order to keep the relationship strong, Dave makes a concerted effort to check back on a monthly basis with each of the primary stakeholders he is supporting, not just the president of the business (which occurs on a much more regular basis), but with the vice presidents and directors, to ensure there is connection and understanding of what is occurring in the business and how HR can provide support. This type of activity takes time and effort, and often causes issues to surface that otherwise might not have surfaced. What it does for Dave is maintain his credibility and retain him as the trusted advisor for the leaders and employees for whom he provides HR support.

When interviewing senior level HR leaders for this book, a key focus was how they effectively and successfully build their relationships with their clients. Whether in pharmaceuticals, retail, transportation, government, information technology or research, all successful and seasoned HR leaders take the time to get to know their clients face-to-face. They go on road trips, make the personal contacts and connections, and spend time in their clients' shoes and in their environments so that they have a deep understanding of the business they are supporting. These trusted HR advisors stress the importance of making personal connections despite the fact that many operate in a virtual world. This behavior builds relationships and begins to form those ideal relationships. Your clients need to believe that you truly understand where they are coming from and are aware of their issues. They need to believe you are their partner and are there to help them succeed. This is most effectively achieved through face-to-face discussions. As much as is reasonably possible, make these connections early on and frequently. Another point to make here is not to do this while fighting fires, and not only when you "have" to be there, but during the course of normal business and when it is not necessarily expected. This is something that a senior HR vice president of a transportation company does regularly. He spends plenty of personal face-to-face time with his clients during the course of normal business, which keeps him in the forefront of his clients' minds as a trusted advisor.

Kevin, an HR vice president with a pharmaceutical company, gave another great example of what he does to work towards his ideal relationships with his clients. He focuses on the "personal" connection by remembering that people have a life outside of their jobs. Kevin's mantra is to "know the human," so he makes an effort to connect early on and finds out about things that are important to them outside of work. You can find out a lot of information in a very unobtrusive manner simply by looking around people's offices at their pictures and what they choose to surround themselves with. Do they have children or pets? Ask them about these things. Do they have a wall calendar with pictures of skiing or running? Chances are they ski or run in their free time. Ask them about these things and get to know them as people in addition to getting to know them as colleagues.

Through the effort of getting to know the whole person, solid relationships begin to form and trust and credibility begin to be established. This brings us back to the point made in the previous chapter about authenticity. It would be very difficult to get to know the "human" and the "whole person" if you did not have the genuine, authentic desire to do so. You probably would not even think of doing this if you weren't truly interested. Yet the most successful and most trusted HR advisors are the ones who never forget the human aspect of their role.

Another example of how HR professionals can achieve that desired end state is to contract with the primary business leader up front; that is, have a discussion with that individual upon taking the assignment (or before hand, if possible) to discuss expectations and decide on the role you will play in supporting the business. For example, Jack was the top candidate for senior vice president of HR position within a $9B company (that was a division of a larger $30B corporation). He had a discussion with the president of the company prior to being offered the position. While on his second round of interviews with the president, Jack had a very candid discussion with her about the role he felt HR should play and the role that he, specifically, would play as the senior HR leader of this company. He told the company president that he wanted to be a partner to the senior leadership team and what that meant to him was that they were all on a level playing field. Jack expressed that he expected honesty and integrity from all the players. This meant that as a team they might not always like what Jack had to say, but he would still speak it and share his opinion in the spirit of honesty, integrity, respect and partnership, and in the spirit of doing what was best for the organization.

Jack specifically told the company president that he would be providing her with open, direct feedback, and that she may not always like or agree with what Jack said, but as her trusted HR advisor, that would be his job. Jack then asked her how she felt about this type of style and interaction from an HR leader, because he needed to gauge whether this relationship would be open and honest or whether it might not ever get off the ground. Jack did this to set the tone and expectations with the primary leader he would be supporting, and he did it before he was even offered the job. He had his end state and ideal relationship in mind, and knew that in order for that vision to be realized and for him to be seen as (and remain) a trusted HR advisor, this type of relationship with the president of the company would be vital. It would also set the tone for how Jack and the rest of his HR team would be perceived throughout that company and it would help the president understand the types of behaviors Jack would be expecting of the HR team that worked for him. All these expectations contributed to a successful long-term relationship between Jack and the company he eventually joined.

The role of HR professionals in building such foundations is to take the initiative and make the effort to get to know the business leaders, key stakeholders, business strategy and objectives for the organization. HR professionals should take these steps and then follow through on necessary actions to provide adequate support. The business leaders also have a role to play in building the foundation of the relationship. The less-than-positive reputation of HR people often hinders a leader's desire to build a relationship. HR professionals cannot control a leader's reactions and responses to their efforts, but they should not alter their path forward in anticipation of a leader's reaction; they should proceed with their objective of building the relationship and being seen as trusted advisors.

Ideally, business leaders will welcome the support and efforts to establish a solid relationship. They will hopefully provide the same type of support, be an equal partner, and instill this approach throughout their organization. They will also hopefully lead by example and seek the advice and counsel of their HR partners when appropriate. This is the end state that has been referenced throughout this chapter. Sometimes this does not occur until after the HR partners demonstrate their trusted advisor behaviors because it takes business leaders time to fully trust in their HR partners. Though it seems obvious that leaders have a responsibility to provide genuine support for their HR partners and do their part to make the relationships work, the reality is that it is incumbent upon the HR professional to initiate the relationship and demonstrate that they will behave and perform as a trusted advisor who understands the business and is acting in support of the company's objectives.

Michael Watkins wrote a book titled, *The First 90 Days: Critical Success Strategies for New Leaders at All Levels.* The first 90 days in a new role is vital, and a time when one can make a great impression and impact. HR professionals should heed this information and the wisdom imparted in Watkins's book. There are a few items highlighted in the book that are worth stating here, as they confirm several of the points previously discussed. Watkins says that in the first 90 days, one should take full responsibility for making new relationships work and clarifying mutual expectations. HR professionals can achieve this in those initial one-on-one meetings and by contracting and negotiating, at the outset, what the key stakeholders' expectations are of their HR partner. Watkins specifically talks about having an "expectations conversation," and although his book speaks about having this conversation with the boss, it can be incredibly useful for

HR professionals to have such a conversation with their clients as well. It will help them understand their clients' needs and objectives as well as what the clients' expectations are of their HR partner.

Watkins references identifying the key players in those first 90 days, because these are the folks who will play a big part in your success. This point echoes the need for HR professionals to do the same to facilitate their success as trusted advisors. Watkins suggests that identifying potential supporters and opponents is essential in your first 90 days. Doing this will enable you to know who will support you no matter what, who might oppose you, and who will either support or oppose you depending on the particular situation. You will then know where you have to spend more time building foundations for strong relationships and who to go to for advocacy.

For example, if you find that there is a senior leader who is always an HR supporter and is well-respected by their peers, this may be a good person for you to use as an advocate for HR programs and initiatives. If you know there is another senior leader who is also respected by his peers but tends to oppose HR initiatives, you know that this is a relationship that might take more time to build. You may need more hard data or spend more time with this person to gain their support. Working on this relationship would be a good place to spend some time in your first 90 days. You may be able to learn why this person opposes HR programs, what their business objectives are and how HR can help. You might want to commit to assisting this person in a particular area and then over-deliver on your commitment in order to turn this opposer into a supporter. Of course, it is not always easy to do this, but it may be time well spent if you can break through the barrier. Taking the time to assess the situation and get to know each of these key stakeholders will provide answers about where you should be spending your time and who may be open for swaying from opposer to supporter.

A great way for structured and organized HR professionals to go about building this foundation and working towards their desired end state is to set up a project plan for the first 90 days in the position. An example of this is included at the end of this chapter and can be completed in any format that one chooses. Begin by listing the items you want to complete and dates by which you want to complete them. Along with scheduling the face-to-face, one-on-one meetings with key stakeholders to find out what their key objectives and issues are, there are some other things to consider doing within the first 90 days: Meet one-on-one with your new staff to begin developing an HR strategy that aligns with the business strategy. Make time to review the developing HR strategy with your key stakeholders to ensure their support and buy-in. Taking that extra step will assist in gaining their consensus as well as show them that your HR strategy has been modeled after all the things you have learned in your first 90-days of getting to know each of them and their businesses. In your 90-day plan you should include specifics such as when you will meet with your key stakeholders and employees, when you will have the business objectives and strategies reviewed, when you will have each key stakeholder's objectives reviewed, when you will have your HR objectives and strategies completed, and when you will share those HR objectives and strategies with the key stakeholders.

An important part of developing ideal relationships with your clients includes understanding what *they* think that ideal relationship includes. Information was gathered from several leaders of Fortune 500 companies about the ideal HR partnership for their organizations and what that partnership looks like and does not look like. The general consensus is that business leaders want an HR partner who understands their specific business needs and who makes an effort to do things that support them reaching their objectives and goals. They want someone who takes the time to understand the issues and who offers solutions instead of roadblocks. They want someone they can trust who gives them credible and useful information and helps them clear a path to a workable solution. They do not want someone who always says "Yes" and they do not want someone who always says "No." They want someone who invests time in getting to know their business, how they run it and their leadership style. Their ideal HR partner trusts that they, as the leaders of the business, know how to run it effectively. Unfortunately, they often find that the relationship is one in which the HR professional primarily plays the role of policy enforcer and has little to say besides "No."

For example, one vice president of a Fortune 100 company, Kate, provided examples about how her experience with HR had typically been filled with condescending interactions and over-exertion of power on the part of HR. Some of these examples will be shared in later sections of this book (where they fit in with a particular Bridge Principle), but for purposes of defining the ideal relationship, let us look at the following example of what an HR person should not do in the first 90 days of trying to build foundations with their clients.

The specific business that Kate was part of had been through a reduction in force several months before their new HR partner came on board. The HR professional, Lauren, was a seasoned woman who had many years of experience, but mostly in the HR specialty of organizational development. Lauren was a woman known for her abrasive personality and somewhat condescending nature. She came into this new role and immediately began making judgments about hiring that was occurring in Kate's department. She felt hiring was not warranted since there had just been a reduction in force three months earlier. Instead of investigating and finding out the reasons for the increased headcount, Lauren took the alternate approach of sending an email to the vice president of HR, the vice president of employment law, the corporate chief information officer and several other high-level people about the fact that Kate was putting the entire corporation at risk by unethically hiring new employees. Kate was not included on the email distribution but she found out about it, and this created the beginning of a very rocky relationship that could never be repaired.

What Lauren did not know was that there were certain areas in the organization in which new hiring was necessary due to changing business needs. These needs had nothing to do with the reduction in force that had occurred several months earlier. Had Lauren taken the time to do some research and find out the details, she might have discovered that no risk was being incurred through the hiring that Kate was doing. What she did was embarrass and isolate one of her key stakeholders very early on in a manner that was detrimental to their long-term relationship. Why she handled the situation this way is unknown, but one can speculate that since she was coming into a role in which some of the content was new and unfamiliar to her, she was looking at the situation in a strictly black-and-white, yes-or-no manner, and looking for what she may have thought of as an early win. What she ended up with was far from a win. Had this truly been a situation in which the corporation was at risk, it could have been a win for Lauren, but, even if it had been a win, handling it differently would have been much more appropriate.

What Lauren should have done was to take a step back and remember that decisions about personnel are not black-and-white but mostly gray; they involve careful consideration and seeking out workable solutions as opposed to policing and looking for what is wrong. As mentioned, unfortunately this relationship could not recover, which highlights the importance of building a solid foundation early on. If the foundation is not stable, it is likely that the relationship will remain shaky at best.

The sentiment from the leaders interviewed for this book is that they clearly want their HR partners to be their trusted advisors, yet struggle because this is not the behavior they see consistently from them. Having an ideal relationship is desirable for both HR professionals and business leaders — a true partnership in which the HR professional understands the business and trusts that the leaders know how to run the business, and in which the HR professional offers advice and counsel that is heeded by the leaders because they know it is being given with the best interests of the business in mind and not as a means to exert power or add complexity to something that is not complicated. It is a relationship in which business leaders seek out their HR partner and want their advice, want them to be part of the decision making, and want them in all the important meetings. This is the desired end state partnership. As you continue to maintain and sustain your relationships with clients, always keep the ideal end state in mind, because even when you get there, or if you are there now, you still have to behave in ways that keep you there and maintain the solidity of the relationship.

"We may be very busy, we may be very efficient, but we will also be truly effective only when we begin with the end in mind."
— STEVEN COVEY

APPLY THIS

Client Contracting Questions

In order to get a full understanding of what your clients expect of you as their HR advisor, use these eight questions to open dialogue with them. Also, answer these questions for yourself to provide the same information back to your clients regarding what you expect of them as you build your relationship. Use these questions as guidance for a two-way discussion so that your clients can share their expectations of you with you and you can share yours with them. This not only serves as a type of informal contract regarding how the relationship will work, but also opens the lines of communication between you and your clients. Note: these questions can be used with any of your clients but often work best when first used with the highest level leader in the organization you support.

1. What has worked well for you in past relationships with HR?

2. What has not worked well?

3. In terms of providing guidance and feedback (When? How? On what topics?), what do you expect of me as your HR advisor?

4. What form of feedback suits you best? (Do you prefer instant feedback? Verbal? Written?)

5. How frequently do you want us to get together one-on-one? Do you want regularly scheduled meetings (Weekly? Bi-weekly?) or impromptu meetings, as needed?

6. What are your expectations of me regarding interacting with your staff and providing them with guidance and counsel?

7. What are your hot issues relative to HR and how can I best support or alleviate them?

8. If I am successful in my role as your trusted HR advisor, what will that look like? What does the end state of our HR/business leader relationship look like to you?

Questions available for download at:
www.trustedadvisorreaderspage.com

First 90-Days: Project Plan

Use this draft project plan as you work through your first 90 days in your role with your clients. Use this even if you are in the middle of an assignment or have been in your assignment for a while and want to reestablish and rebuild that trusted relationship.

TASK	TIME FRAME FOR COMPLETION	RESPONSIBLE PARTY	DESIRED OUTCOME
One-on-one meetings with senior level leader.	First 2 weeks	HR Advisor	Discuss contracting questions.
One-on-one meetings with senior level staff.	First 60 days	HR Advisor	Introduction/re-introduction; discuss/determine leaders top priorities and top 3 HR issues.
Share outcome of meetings with team of direct reports or with HR leadership (as appropriate).	First 75 days	HR Advisor, HR Team, HR Leadership	Ensure HR leadership and your HR team understand your clients' top priorities and top HR concerns.
Develop HR action plan that outlines how HR will work with clients most effectively.	First 90 days	HR Advisor, HR Team	Outline and documentation of how you, as HR advisor, and your team will best work with and support your clients.
Communicate action plan with senior business leaders of client group.	By end of first 90 days	HR Advisor	Obtain feedback from business leaders on path forward and ensure their buy-in on path forward.

Template available for download at:
www.trustedadvisorreaderspage.com

"Though no one can go back and make a brand new start, anyone can start from now and make a brand new ending."

~ ANONYMOUS

AUTHOR'S NOTE:
PRINCIPLE I

One of my clients, an HR director, started to support a new business leader in her organization. Although she had known him for many years in other roles and had worked well with him in the past, she was now struggling to develop a solid relationship with him. He took over as the vice president and general manager of the organization she supported, and she was now providing him primary HR support. Therefore, a new dynamic emerged between them and the old rules governing how they had worked together in former roles were no longer in place. I coached her through the process of essentially starting anew with him. I suggested that she act as if she had never known him and treat him as if he were a brand new leader in the organization. We worked together on some ways she could effectively utilize the Build Your Base concepts and negotiate a new partnership contract with him. This has enabled them to work successfully together in these new roles. She is now coaching him through some road bumps he has encountered in his transition to this higher-level position and it started with her own efforts to rewind and go back to build a solid base relationship with him, one that now enables her to be a coach and trusted advisor to him.

RESPOND RESPONSIBLY

To respond responsibly is to take ownership for your responses; it is to have an open heart and mind as you begin to communicate with others. Doing this encourages exploration, the flow of ideas and a desire to reach shared goals. To respond responsibly and openly is to put thought into what is said prior to it being said. To respond in this way is to not react.

CHAPTER 3

HOW DO YOU COMMUNICATE?

WHEN YOU THINK ABOUT HOW TO COMMUNICATE WITH others, do you first think about what outcome you are trying to achieve? Do you think about the result you want to achieve from what you are saying and doing? Or do you just speak without filtering anything? Unless someone is communicating a message that they have rehearsed, they do not typically listen to or think about how they sound. They do not take the time to consider their tone or demeanor prior to speaking. The tone with which we verbally communicate says a lot about the message we are trying to get across. Soft tones tell a very different story than harsh tones, even if the same words are coming out of one's mouth. Tones also infer demeanor. When talking with a severe tone to someone on the phone, your demeanor can be interpreted as defensive or abrasive, whereas when you speak with a soft tone, it can be inferred that your demeanor is calm or gentle.

HR professionals need to consider their desired outcome prior to communicating their message to clients. It is often necessary to send a difficult message by adopting a strict tone that infers a serious demeanor. Other times it is more effective to use a tone that is softer and infers a calm demeanor.

An example of this occurred in a senior leadership meeting in which Meredith, an HR director, was trying to provide her clients (the corporate chief operating officer and his staff of vice presidents) with feedback about the considerable number of performance issues and discipline cases that had occurred over the past twelve months. Meredith's desired outcome was for the leadership teams to take action sooner and be more responsible in managing these issues as opposed to ignoring them until they ended up as discipline cases. Her tone and demeanor did not assist in reaching this outcome. She spoke in a harsh tone, very forcefully, with a glare in her eyes, as she told them, "The number of egregious violations that have been occurring over the past year is outrageous and the managers should be ashamed that they have not been dealing with these issues before they become ethical violations." Instead of gaining support from the leadership team, Meredith isolated them because they interpreted her message as scolding, condescending and parental. They did not know how to reply to that type of message, so what occurred was silence, and then the meeting moved on to another topic so the subject was never fully addressed. Worse than that, Meredith actually believed that her message got through to them. She took their silence as agreement and understanding. The better approach might have been for Meredith to think beforehand about the best tone and demeanor to use with this group to ensure that her message achieved the desired result. If she had actually heard how she sounded, she might have been a bit embarrassed by the tone and then understood the resulting silence from the leadership team.

Do you know how you sound? Stop and listen to yourself the next time you are communicating. Do you know what your own communication style is and how it impacts those around you? There are a variety of communication styles, yet people are often classified as either an aggressive, passive or assertive communicator.

The example above is one of an aggressive communicator - one who is outspoken, does not listen well, does not consider others' feelings or perceptions when communicating, and is domineering, bossy and condescending. This type of style would not bode well for a trusted HR advisor because it does not invite open communication.

A passive communicator is the opposite of an aggressive communicator. This person typically agrees with others, does not speak up, does not exude confidence when speaking, is hesitant, and does not like to make waves. This type of style also would not bode well for a trusted HR advisor because someone who is trusted by their clients should feel confident and comfortable being honest with them. Even if they are giving their clients information that is not what their clients want to hear, they are confident and comfortable because it is the information that is in the best interests of the business.

As an HR professional, the best communication style is one that is often referred to as assertive. Assertiveness is sometimes associated with being forceful, so a better way of describing the style of a trusted HR advisor is confident and self-assured. This person is an active listener and clearly states expectations as well as limits. They are non-judgmental, open, flexible and decisive. It is important for HR professionals to know what their communication style is and, regardless of whether it is passive or aggressive, to work towards becoming a confident and self-assured communicator.

If we go back to the prior example and alter Meredith's communication style to that of a confident and self-assured communicator, the message would be drastically different. If she had considered that the desired outcome was to obtain the leaders' assistance with and ownership of these issues, she might have approached them differently. By using a calm demeanor and posing questions regarding whether or not they were aware of the performance and discipline problems, she would have gotten a better response. Then, depending on their response, she could have presented them with some factual data regarding how many violations there had been and the degree of severity of the violations. Again, by using the collaborative, partnering approach of a confident communicator, Meredith could have presented them with some options and suggestions for how to deal with these situations. She could also have asked them for their input to get a full understanding about what they were willing to commit to and accept responsibility for regarding this situation. There would not have been any blame placed on the leaders. Trusted advisors should and would approach the leaders from a place of wanting to partner and help them, and from a place of being on the same side, instead of scolding and blaming them.

Another point to think about when communicating and responding to clients is the timing of your responses and how this contributes to and supports your communication style. Do you respond instantly or do you wait before responding? Most people think about whom they need to respond to prior to deciding whether to do it immediately or to wait. However, the instant response is not always recommended for a trusted HR advisor. Responding instantly can often be construed as reacting, and contributes to the perception that HR professionals are roadblocks and naysayers, especially if those instant responses include words like no, can't or don't.

For example, imagine you receive an email from a client that indicates that there is a need for support from the HR department to hire 50 people within the next week to staff a key program that was just awarded. The instant response to that request could easily be, "That is something that cannot be done." Now, this example is a bit of an exaggeration because typically an organization or a specific department within an organization would have some form of work-force planning in place and there would have been arrangements made in advance to staff such a program. However, the point here is that it is very easy to drop the instant response of "No" when it seems so obvious. Yet if you wait before responding, take the time to consider the reason for the statement or request, and explore alternative options, then the response might be something different. If you still feel compelled to respond instantly, responding with, "Tell me more," or, "I need some more information; can we discuss this further?" would be a more appropriate instant response.

HR professionals are often so bombarded with questions and requests that the instant "No" response is an easy way to get something off their plate or get an email out of the inbox. Yet the consequence of the quick "No" is often a perception that HR personnel are naysayers and roadblocks. Are there any positives to responding instantly? Perhaps, in that those who respond instantly are deemed responsive. But what about the quality of those responses? Are they well thought out and informative? Are they giving the client the level of information that has been requested and is required? Responding immediately can also be equated to not pausing long enough to reflect on the most suitable reply. It is better to pause and reflect on the most appropriate answer to a question, so although being known as responsive is a positive characteristic for an HR professional to have, it should not be the reason for instant replies.

The flip side of this topic is to consider how a delayed response is perceived and the benefits of taking your time to respond. Delaying a response, in the context of this topic, means waiting long enough so you have had sufficient time to formulate the appropriate response, as suited to a trusted HR advisor. Pause long enough to allow yourself time to consider your clients, their goals, and what they are trying to achieve prior to giving them the answer or information they are seeking. This delay would not apply to questions such as, "How many paid, fixed holidays do we get this year?" or, "How much vacation time are new hires given?" The delayed response applies to requests that require HR professionals to partner with their clients and determine the best solution for their specific needs, such as in the example above.

Bernard M. Baruch (1870-1965) is quoted as saying, "Whatever failures I have known, whatever errors I have committed, whatever follies I have witnessed in private and public life have been the consequence of action without thought." To be trusted advisors, HR professionals should be thoughtful prior to acting and prior to responding. Just as you should consider the desired outcome of verbal communication and listen to how you sound when speaking, you should also consider the desired outcome of the instant response, both in verbal and in written form.

This brings us to the next item in the area of communication, which is how to respond. When is it appropriate to respond verbally, in writing, or both? First consider the type of interaction you are looking for and whether or not it needs a personal touch. Phone calls and live conversations can generate more understanding between the parties involved because there is actual human interaction. With email or any other written reply, this aspect is missing. In today's business world, email exchanges typically take the lead over verbal communication. Everyone has a Blackberry, iPhone or some other handheld device that makes replying while in a meeting, while on a conference call, or while on a train or in an airport much easier than trying to call someone and have a conversation. Many people prefer written communication for the pure ease of it. Others (especially extraverts) prefer a quick phone call or conversation to an email exchange. But for ease and speed of response, emails, text messages and instant messages are more commonly used today.

If we go back to the original question about how much of a personal touch is needed, that is a decision you need to make based on the information at hand. For example, Matthew, an HR professional, recently received a draft email from Sarah, one of his HR colleagues who had been working on a project with a few senior vice presidents. Sarah was distraught that the project was falling behind schedule because the business leaders were delinquent in returning data that was vital to the project's outcome. The project schedule had already slipped several times before this particular event. The prior delays had been due to the HR team's challenges with their part of the project. Now the schedule was going to slip again, however this time it was because of the leaders' delinquency. Sarah wanted to send an email to the vice presidents she was working with and let them know that the project schedule was slipping because of their department leaders' being late with data collection. She asked Matthew to review the email prior to her sending it. Thank goodness she did. The first sentence read, "Four of your departments are late getting their data back to me and because of that, the project schedule will slip yet again." Matthew was surprised at the bluntness of the first sentence and as he continued to read on, it became more and more clear that the email would completely isolate these business leaders from Sarah (even more than they were already isolated), as the email was focused on placing blame. The recommendation from Matthew was that perhaps a phone conversation with these vice presidents would yield a better result. Sarah could voice her concern that based on some late responses, the project would slip and that she wanted to discuss alternatives to ensure they proceeded on the best path forward to meet the deadline. Again, as with the first example in this chapter, the approach of the trusted advisor should include an attitude of partnering and collaborating and not one of placing blame. Placing blame isolates clients from their human resources partners, and that is something that HR professionals do not want to do.

The general rule of thumb regarding email versus discussion should be this: Touchy topics require personal touches. This is common practice among trusted HR advisors in all industries. If the topic is sensitive or heated in any way, or if there is potential for misunderstanding via email, pick up the phone and have a conversation. Email subtleties are very difficult to interpret correctly, even if you know the person well. Pick up the phone and have a conversation whenever there are more than three back-and-forth emails. Pick up the phone and have a conversation whenever you feel the need to capitalize any of the words in your email. Yes, it is okay to capitalize or highlight words if you are emphasizing a due date or time frame that must be met, but it is not okay if you are highlighting other types of words in your email. People tend to interpret email based on how they are feeling instead of on how the sender is feeling. Email should be used to communicate factual information, gather necessary factual or objective data, and provide factual, objective assistance. It should not be used to communicate sensitive issues, gather subjective opinions or gain consensus. Those are the kinds of personal touch issues that require a conversation.

There are some more general rules-of-thumb for email. First, do not copy it to others unnecessarily, and second, never send a nasty email. Even if you make the mistake of doing that, be sure not to copy anyone else in on it; you will embarrass yourself more than the recipient of the nasty email. Typically when this happens, the sender of the scathing email is seen as the wrongdoer as opposed to the recipient. For example, a senior HR leader, Ann, was the recipient of a scathing email. This email, with copies sent to several other people, was not only off-base in regard to the accusations, but also included bolded, capitalized letters: "**YOU** and **YOUR TEAM** had no right to share any information on the departmental realignment with **MY**

business leaders." The story behind this was that Ann, a senior HR leader, and her team, were delivering information about a sizeable department redesign to many different sites in their large company. Samantha, who sent the email, was another senior HR leader who had been out of the office and was not aware of the communication plan and the schedule to communicate the changes. She incorrectly placed blame upon Ann for doing exactly what was supposed to be done. Had Samantha first caught up on her own open items prior to sending the scathing email, she would have realized that no wrong had been done. Instead she reacted, sent the email, and sent copies not only to many of her peers, but also to a couple of senior level HR leaders who were all up to date on the appropriate communication schedule. Clearly Samantha appeared uninformed and reactive by acting this way, and was very embarrassed after realizing the facts behind the situation. So, again, thinking before acting, and deciding what the desired outcome should be, can assist in avoiding this kind of communication blunder.

Communication is much more than writing or speaking; it is also nonverbal. HR professionals should keep in mind the messages they are sending through nonverbal cues. For example, do you sit in your office with your door closed even when you are not on the phone or having a confidential conversation? If so, you might want to think about the message this sends. While you may need to close your door on occasion in order to concentrate, an open door demonstrates your availability to your clients. If your door is closed all the time, you may be perceived as unavailable or unwilling and unable to provide support or information. Planning for "open door" time is as important as planning for "closed door" time to accomplish tasks. The key is to have balance and ensure that you are available and open to your clients so that they feel comfortable coming to you with their HR issues.

In addition to the subtle messages sent by nonverbal actions such as a consistently closed office door, when trusted advisors are facilitating or participating in meetings and interactions with their clients, they need to be especially aware of nonverbal cues in their posture, stance and facial expressions. Keeping in mind Principle I regarding authenticity and being genuine, checking your nonverbal cues may seem like a non-authentic thing to do. After all, if you are being genuine and feel like you just heard the most ridiculous comment ever, then why not roll your eyes, throw your arms up and try to hold in a snicker? Wouldn't that be genuine? Well, yes, it would, but remember you are trying to build a bridge that supports your clients' needs and get them to trust you, as opposed to isolating them. The authenticity that was discussed in Chapter 1 is about your genuine desire to help your clients. The idea of keeping your nonverbal cues in check is not being inauthentic, but is a part of building that bridge and developing the trust that your clients seek from you.

Melinda, an HR director at a large Fortune 500 company, was facilitating a meeting for her colleagues. It was a group of HR directors and vice presidents who were meeting to calibrate the performance ratings of their teams. There were some tense moments in the meeting because there were differing opinions about some of the employees' performance. At one point during the meeting there were the following postures around the room: one person had her elbows on the table and her face in her hands, one person was sitting in his chair with his arms crossed and had a very stern look on his face, one person was working on her laptop, and another was leaning back in his chair with a smirk on his face and his hands clasped behind his head. Melinda had actually put her own hands in her pockets. With the exception of the individual who was leaning back in his chair and smirking, everyone else appeared to be quite closed off to the discussion. Arms folded, hands in pockets, and face in hands are all signals of being closed off from the discussion and not open to new ideas. The individual who was leaning back in his chair with a smirk on his face was actually getting ready to leave the company for a new opportunity, so he was amused by the stressful discussion, and it was obvious through his nonverbal cues – he was relaxed and nonchalant. Melinda felt overwhelmed by the reaction she was getting from her peers; hence she had her hands in her pockets, which is typically a signal that someone is not open to talking. Obviously, that is not a good stance for a facilitator to use. Folding arms sends the signal of being unapproachable and can reduce your credibility as a trusted advisor. Rolling your eyes sends the message that you believe you are better than or that you know more than the person you rolled your eyes at, or perhaps that you have no patience for them.

The meeting participants were actually unaware of their posture, stance and facial expressions. In fact, it was a videotaped meeting so they were able to replay and review their discussion. When they did so, they were all surprised and also amused at their own nonverbal cues. They were not aware that they were conveying such strong messages to each other even though they were not saying anything verbally.

The message here is that you should be aware of your posture and stance and your facial expressions when you are consulting with your leaders, coaching your leaders and employees, or coaching and interacting with your peers. You might have the best of intentions and the genuine desire to help and assist your clients, yet you can send the opposite message through the simple act of rolling your eyes at one of their questions or standing with your arms folded as they are sharing concerns with you. If you make this mistake in front of them, acknowledge it immediately and apologize. Be aware of how you are feeling internally and how this is being expressed externally. Keep your body language in check so it does not undermine your desire to be a trusted advisor.

To conclude this very important topic of how you communicate, if you do only one thing to improve your behavior in this area, it should be this: Pay attention and pause. Pay attention to what you are thinking and feeling and how this might impact what you are saying and doing, and pause before you speak. Take a breath and keep in mind what you are trying to achieve through what you are going to say. This will most certainly increase your chances of communicating in an effective manner and responding responsibly, as opposed to reacting in a way that could potentially isolate your clients.

> *"Reacting is taking action without conscious awareness or analysis. Responding is making a decision with the involvement of a conscious choice."*
>
> ~ ANONYMOUS

CHAPTER 4

ADVANCE RESPONDING

THE WAY IN WHICH HR PROFESSIONALS SOMETIMES react (instead of respond) is often the result of being overwhelmed with a constant flow of questions and concerns from the clients they support. The examples of what not to do when communicating that were shared in the previous chapter often occur because of this feeling of being overwhelmed. One way to thwart the constant flow of questions and concerns is to have a method of "advance responding". To respond in advance means that you already have a communication plan in place for sharing vital HR related information with your clients. Although this will not eliminate the need for personal contact and interaction, and will not eliminate their questions and need for answers, it will most certainly reduce the kinds of requests that can inundate you. Your clients will know many of the answers to their questions because of your advanced communication. Something quite simple can actually enable you to invest your energy more strategically and have the time to practice your trusted advisor behaviors instead of being in firefighting mode. It will also enable you to respond responsibly.

An "HR Communication Plan" spells out what, when and how you will communicate pertinent HR information to your clients. The HR Communication Plan should include your HR calendar of events and, as with any HR-related initiative, both should line up with the business rhythm in your company and the calendar of strategic business events. The first step in this process is to ensure that your HR calendar of events aligns with your business's calendar of events. Keeping in mind what you discovered in Principle I about building your base, you should be aware of your business's primary objectives and be able to map out your HR events as they relate to the business events. For example, many business leaders communicate the overarching business objectives to their workforce in the first quarter of the year. At this time the HR department often establishes its performance management process and sets forth the initiative for all employees to set individual performance objectives for the year. They communicate the specific HR initiative (which is for the workforce to set individual performance objectives) that is in support of the business objective (which is the rollout of the business's annual objectives). This is the "what" piece of the HR Communication Plan.

The next part of the plan is the how and who. How to communicate this most effectively, and to whom in the workforce, will depend entirely upon the size of the business you support, the culture, and the communication channels that need to be followed. For a large company, there is often a communications department that handles these types of tasks. Or, the HR leaders communicate the requirement directly to the leaders in their particular departments and then mass emails with more specific details are distributed to the entire workforce. In a smaller company, you may be communicating at an all-hands meeting (either live or virtually, via webcast) during which the business leaders share the overarching business objectives to the entire workforce and then HR communicates the requirements for individual objective-setting. The recipients of the communication would be the entire workforce because all employees will have responsibility for setting objectives that their performance will then be managed against. The overarching HR Communication Plan includes this type of information for each HR initiative that needs to be communicated to the workforce (or a subset of the workforce). Having this in place at the beginning of each year enables you, as the trusted HR advisor, to distribute it to your clients so they know what the key HR programs are for the year, when they will occur, and when information about the HR programs will be communicated. A sample HR calendar of events is included in the "Apply This" section for Principle II at the end of this chapter.

There is a two-part example of how this advance communication practice helped support an HR department in being able respond responsibly – how it enabled them to focus their time and attention in the right places as well as thwart some of the endless tactical questions that come up. The first part of the example looks at how overwhelmed an HR team can become when operating in an environment in which there is no HR Communication Plan in place. The second part of the example turns this scenario around by implementing a plan.

This example comes from a technology company with approximately 2,500 employees that expanded rapidly over a three-year period. They did not devote focused time to enhancing their HR department and expanding it along with the growth in other areas of the company. The same three HR professionals who had been supporting 500 employees five years earlier were now supporting 2,500 employees. That being said, you can imagine that there was not a lot of time to be strategic and plan ahead. There was also a significant amount of reacting that went on instead of responsible responding. This team of HR professionals was simply trying to keep up to make sure the company was in compliance with employment law and procedural regulations, that employees were paid, and that performance was being managed adequately. But because they did not have an HR agenda, calendar or communication plan, they were constantly running around fighting fires. They were continually overwhelmed with questions about payroll, health insurance and a myriad other tactical issues – so much so that they could do little more than sit in their offices all day long and respond to phone calls, visits from employees and email requests. This created a lot of stress for them. They did not have the time or energy to be strategic and were often frustrated with the workforce simply because they were at their breaking point. What they really wanted was to be able to refer their clients to the specific policy or procedure that had the answers to their questions, but the employees did not even know where to access that information.

Finally, Dan, the HR director of this small HR team, made a decision to first align the HR team's priorities with the business priorities. This included hiring on a few more HR professionals so that the HR team could support the growing workforce more effectively. Next Dan decided to publish an annual HR calendar of events so that the entire workforce would know when certain HR initiatives were to occur throughout the year. The first pass of this calendar included the major HR items that would impact the workforce. For example, it informed employees that in the first quarter the performance objective-setting period began. In the second quarter, managers would hold career discussions with employees. In the third quarter, open enrollment for benefits occurred. In the fourth quarter, performance appraisals were to be completed and merit increases were to be given.

Dan then instructed his HR team to put together an HR Communication Plan to publish along with a corresponding HR calendar of events so that, for example, prior to performance objective-setting, a previously scheduled email communication went out to all leaders and all employees with the details about what was required of them. The plan also included information about the training that was available for new employees and new leaders about setting performance objectives and when it would be conducted. It included details about the timing of training that would be provided for leaders prior to holding career discussions in the second quarter (so that they had knowledge of how to conduct an effective discussion with employees), as well as when the email would be distributed to leaders with specific details about the timeframe within which they were required to hold these discussions. It also included the dates when employees would receive their annual benefits open enrollment information, when annual performance appraisal discussions would be held, and when merit increases would go into effect. By publishing the HR calendar of events, employees were less apt to inundate the HR team with questions because they already had many of the answers.

The team decided to also launch a mass HR Communication Plan regarding HR policies and procedures. In order to make employees aware of the various HR policies and procedures and educate them about how to access the information, they sent out bi-weekly emails over a three month period to introduce and re-introduce employees to the information available to them and accessible via their company intranet. Again, this small action opened up an entirely new avenue that employees could use to get the information they needed. Instead of inundating HR with petty and time-consuming questions and requests, employees were able to access it on their own. This eased the stress on Dan and his HR team and freed up their time to be more strategic and begin working on the key items aligned with being trusted advisors. It also eased their frustration and tendency to react to some of the tactical questions that had been consistently coming their way.

Another key aspect to consider along with the HR Communication Plan is the best communication method to use for each piece of the plan. Certain types of communication are best done via email (for example, the mass messaging that needs to go out to 2,500 employees in the prior example). However, there are elements of an HR Communication Plan that work best through direct verbal communication. HR professionals might meet face-to-face with the business leaders either in staff meetings, in a large group, or on a webcast to provide them with information that is specific to their responsibilities in regard to HR items. For instance, they would communicate the leaders' required duties for the performance management cycle, and for conducting career discussions with employees, as well as other pertinent items.

In larger companies where certain HR functions are centralized and company-wide HR initiatives need to flow out to field HR professionals, there would be tiered HR communication plans. The centralized (or corporate) HR function would have an HR Communication Plan that includes specifics about communicating to senior executives and then to field HR representatives in regard to the timing and scheduling of their particular HR program. The field HR professionals would then design their HR Communication Plan as the next tier down from the corporate one.

For example, in a large retail company, the corporate learning and development team sets the implementation schedule and communication plan for the talent-planning process. This team communicates to the senior corporate leaders and the field HR teams what the enterprise-wide requirements for talent-planning will be and what types of communication will be sent out. The communication methods include briefings to the senior leaders, emails to the entire leadership population and emails to employees – all specifying what will be happening and what leaders' and employees' responsibilities are in regard to these items. In turn, the field HR teams develop their specific communication plans for their division's workforce so that it aligns with the corporate plan as well as their specific division's plan. The field team may have additional items to communicate and in a slightly different manner, based on their specific division's structure and needs, but it will all line up with and coordinate with the overall HR Communication Plan from the corporate team.

In even larger companies, there is typically a representative from the communications department who supports the HR department and coordinates all types of HR communications, including those regarding performance management, talent management, compensation, benefits, and any other related HR program. These overarching communications would be distributed throughout the organization in a similar fashion as described previously. The key point here is that for consistency purposes, the field HR professionals tailor the communications plans to their specific division's needs yet always mirror the overall corporate communication plan.

Circulating advance communications via an HR Communication Plan, though it may seem cumbersome, will definitely decrease unnecessary questions and save time in the HR department. Another key element is that it should be a continuous and flexible plan. A large HR team in a 40,000-person healthcare company has a practice of updating the leadership team on the HR calendar of events and pertinent upcoming items, minimally, on a monthly basis. Some HR professionals update the business leaders they support on a more frequent basis via staff meetings. The review of the HR calendar of events is a standing agenda item during staff meetings and is one that is supported by the business leaders. Those HR leaders who do not have staff meetings with their business leaders as frequently conduct a monthly update with their business leadership team. This is detailed as part of the HR Communication Plan and ensures that the business leaders are receiving a constant flow of information on pertinent HR items and initiatives that are on the horizon. The HR Communication Plan also includes monthly emails to the workforce to inform those who are not in leadership roles of pertinent HR items that are forthcoming and will impact them. This, again, provides a consistent flow of information and the advance communication that assists with and supports the trusted HR advisor's behavior of responding responsibly.

A practice such as this also allows for some flexibility in the HR calendar of events and making adjustments as necessary. A good example of this comes from a pharmaceutical company that has a similar practice in place. The HR calendar is reviewed with their business leadership teams at regular staff meetings. During a meeting with the most senior leadership team, the senior HR vice president, Ted, was communicating the plans for a new workforce planning process and associated training that was to be distributed to the entire enterprise-wide leadership team over the course of the next few months. This was an initiative that was originally agreed upon, earlier in the year, as supportive of the business objectives. However, since that time, some key business events had occurred which were shifting the focus for the leaders. This prompted a discussion about delaying the workforce planning initiative and replacing it with strategic sales force development which was necessitated in the short term due to the recent change in business priorities. The senior executives agreed to alter the original HR training initiatives and delay the workforce planning process implementation.

Ted then convened his HR leadership team to work on a plan to execute the sales force development while pushing the workforce planning initiative off until later that year. The HR calendar of events was adjusted accordingly and communications flowed out to the company leaders as appropriate. This is a great example of how the use of an HR Communication Plan can facilitate the smooth flow of designing and altering HR objectives and programs to best support business priorities.

It is also important to remember that communication comes in a variety of forms: verbal, written, formal, informal, educational, etc. For each form there are electronic types of communication and live, face-to-face types of communication. It is essential that the HR Communication Plan for your organization fit best with your culture and how your business operates. You should ensure that you are communicating via avenues that are utilized by all. For example, younger employees are apt to use electronic types of communication exclusively, whereas others may prefer to receive their communication verbally or face-to-face. If your workforce is diverse, a variety of methods should be used to communicate with them.

It is also essential to consider the subject and how elaborate or extensive the communication needs to be. If you are introducing a new HR program or something that will be a change for your company culture, you will likely need to develop a more extensive HR Communication Plan to support that initiative. If you are communicating the upcoming holiday schedule, an email to the workforce is probably sufficient. The key is ensuring that your HR Communication Plan maps to your business rhythm, supports your key business and HR objectives, and supports your company culture so that communications are well-received and understood. This is a vital aspect of ensuring that HR professionals in your organization are able to respond responsibly more often than not.

"To effectively communicate, we must realize that we are all different in the way we perceive the world and use this understanding as a guide to our communication with others."

~ UNKNOWN

APPLY THIS

The Two-Hour Challenge

For the next month, any time you get an email or a voice mail that elicits a feeling of wanting to reply instantly, wait two hours and then respond. If you feel compelled to respond immediately, draft a response at that time, but do not send it. Put it in a draft document, wait two hours and then send the email or return the phone call. Chances are that 50% of the time you will revise your response. If not, then you validated that you had the right response from the start. Regardless, your answer will be the responsible response of a trusted advisor. Try this practice for a month and if it works well, continue to use it until you develop a habit of pausing prior to responding.

Two-Hour Challenge Journal Template available for download at:
www.trustedadvisorreaderspage.com

HR Calendar of Events

Below is a sample template for you to use as your HR Calendar of Events which should correspond to your HR Communication Plan. There are a few examples included to get you started in putting yours together.

Sample HR Calendar of Events

Month	HR Program	Corresponding Business Objective	Completion Timeframe	To Whom?	Date
Jan.	Setting Performance Objectives	Managing workforce performance	Jan 15-March 31	All Leaders	Jan 1-15
				All leaders and employees	Jan. 10
Feb.	Time and attendance policy updates	Controlling overhead expenditures and paid time off	Feb. 28	All leaders and employees	Feb. 15

Ideally, this calendar and communication plan would be shared with leaders starting in December of the prior year so they have advance communication regarding when they will be receiving important information on pertinent HR Programs. The events that take place over the course of several months (such as Setting Performance Objectives) would remain on the calendar and on regular staff meeting agendas for discussion as well as for reminder purposes while it is an active item. Once an item has been completed, it can be removed from the calendar or indicated as complete.

You might want to have a separate document similar to the one above for each month of the year depending on how many items are on the calendar.

Sample HR Calendar of Events Template available for download at: **www.trustedadvisorreaderspage.com**

AUTHOR'S NOTE: PRINCIPLE II

I worked with a client in the area of responding responsibly in regard to his communication style. He was a very passive communicator and this was not effective for him in his role as an HR leader in his organization. He wanted to shift his style to one of a self-assured and confident communicator.

He was extremely smart, well-spoken and considered a high-potential employee. However, due to cultural norms within which he was raised, he had a difficult time communicating in a self-assured manner, especially to leaders at higher levels in the organization. His passive style was keeping others from having confidence in him as a trusted HR advisor and he knew he needed to be more assured in his communication style if he were to have the respect of his leadership and the clients he supported.

We worked together on creating a style that felt good and was authentic for him. Clearly, if he tried something that was outside of his realm of authenticity, he would not be able to sustain it. We did a lot of real-time coaching in which I would observe him in meeting settings and provide him with some immediate feedback and coaching about what he might try to do differently. He experimented with a variety of different approaches and we did a lot of role-playing until he came into a style that was truly his own. It was not what he felt he "had" to do based on his upbringing and it was not what he felt he "had" to do to fit the mold of the perfect HR communicator; it was his own style of confidence in which he felt genuine conviction about what he was communicating to his leadership team. The more he practiced this style, the more confident he grew about his communications which translated into increased confidence from his leadership team.

INFLUENCE
IMPECCABLY

To influence impeccably is to do so without flaw or fault. It is to exert your influence skills in a manner that has value, meaning, and a direct, positive impact on your clients and their goals and objectives. It is to be clear and immaculate in what you are saying and how you are saying it, as well as in what you are doing and how you are doing it. To influence impeccably is to know what, where, when and how. It is an art and a practice that needs to be mastered by trusted advisors.

CHAPTER 5

INFLUENCING AND INSERTING

I F YOU HAVE BEEN PRACTICING THE FIRST AND second Bridge Principles, have built your base with your clients, have a solid foundation in place with them, and are communicating with them in the best possible and most effective manner, then you have earned the right to insert yourself and begin to influence their actions and decisions. It is not only your privilege at this point, but also your responsibility as a trusted advisor. The definition of influence is "the capacity or power of persons or things to be a compelling force on or produce effects on the actions, behavior, opinions, etc., of others" (dictionary.com, 2010). Influencing impeccably really means inserting yourself in a manner that is not seen as intrusive or overstepping boundaries. It is to be an active participant and fully engaged with your clients. It is to use your best behaviors to have a direct and powerful impact on the clients and businesses you support. So how exactly do you influence impeccably?

As you begin to practice influencing, you should keep a few vital influencing skills in mind. The first thing to do is go back to the concept discussed in Principle I, which is to begin with the end in mind. Determine where you want to go versus where you are, and then decide what needs to be done to get from here to there. By having this end state in mind, you can use these next steps to effectively influence your clients in order to get there.

Next, listen. Most people think of listening as a passive act, but it actually is one of the most active and critical influencing skills. You will not be able to influence your clients (or anyone, for that matter) without truly listening to their needs and their perspectives. Repeat what they say so you are sure you truly understand where they are coming from and they are sure you heard what they said. When you repeat back to your client (or anyone you are looking to influence) exactly what they said in the language they said it, they instantly know that you heard them and were listening. They are likely to think, "They get it!"

The next thing to do is put yourself in their shoes. It sounds cliché but it truly works. Just think to yourself, "What would I do if I were sitting where they are?" Thinking from their perspective (and not your own) will be enlightening, and you may give voice to your suggestions slightly differently than if you had not tried to see the situation from their viewpoint.

The last step is to go back to listening. However, this time you should listen to yourself. In the spirit of continued authenticity, listen to your gut and your heart and how you feel about the situation. This can and will guide your influence and the suggestions you make to your clients in the most genuine manner. Being genuine makes for much more effective influence than being disingenuous.

There are many examples to share about how successful, trusted HR advisors use these techniques (and many others) to exert impeccable influence. One example includes the use of data and speaking your client's language when trying to influence them. Dave, the HR vice president in a transportation and shipping company, needed to influence his business leaders to support the use of a new performance management system. Although this was something the leaders knew that they needed, getting them to support it and hold their teams accountable for implementation during a very busy year required excellent influencing skills. Dave knew that he was dealing with leaders who were very data and numbers-driven (as most are). To feed their hunger for data, he used statistics and hard numbers to show that by taking the time to implement the new system and process that year, the time spent on performance management in the coming years would be reduced by approximately 16%. It would also increase the efficiency with which poor performers would be managed out of the business. Dave did not speak about HR-specific things such as increased employee engagement and better differentiation of high and low-performing talent, but instead spoke in terms the leaders understood and which resonated with them: less time having to be spent on performance management in the future meant more time available for growing the business, meeting with customers and improving services. By spending time with leaders and clients to learn how their world operates and how to speak their language, you increase your ability to influence them in an impeccable manner.

This is also true in the pharmaceutical and healthcare industry. Tony is the vice president of talent management at a well-known pharmaceutical and medical devices company. He finds that he is most effective influencing senior leaders when he has hard numbers to share with them. He uses data to demonstrate how talent management and development programs impact the business. Tony also uses numbers to demonstrate that investing in the development of high-potential employees increases their promotion rate and enables them to have a greater and more positive impact on the business. If

Tony has this type of data available to share with his senior leaders, he knows that it will add to his ability to influence them in supporting a new leadership assessment and development program. If your client's language is laden with data and hard numbers, then you need to include that language in your own discussions with them to exert influence impeccably.

Another example is in the area of listening. This becomes especially important if you are experiencing resistance from your clients. Carole is an HR leader in a large research firm and often finds that her clients resist change because they are scientists and very much focused on their research and design work. Yet Carole also knows that resistance from her clients often occurs as a result of pressure to meet deadlines and perform within constrained budgets. Therefore, she makes a concerted effort to work closely with them on a consistent and regular basis to support them in their efforts to meet tight deadlines. She is present, working with them or checking in with them as much as possible, even when there is nothing HR-related occurring. This enables her to have a full understanding of their pressure points; she can lend support or alternative suggestions if they resist a very important businesses-focused HR initiative.

As an HR professional and trusted advisor, you should listen, ask questions, and do your very best to understand where resistance is coming from. You should attempt to stand in your clients' shoes so that you can use appropriate suggestions and language that resonates with them and ultimately will influence them. By using this technique of consistently working closely with your clients, regardless of whether there is an HR situation going on or not, you also build your credibility.

Sam, the HR vice president of a Fortune 500 technology company, uses this method to help with his influencing skills. Sam knows that by consistently being present with his clients, they know he will be there for them and they believe that he truly understands them. They trust that he will go to battle for them and do what is best for them. Using this practice will make it much easier to exert influence on your clients and increase their respect for you.

Another example in the area of listening deals with listening to yourself. Frank is an HR director in a large government contracting company and he uses self-awareness to assist in exerting influence. He feels that he must know his own style and that of the person or persons he is trying to influence in order to be able to do so effectively. Understanding your own style allows you to determine whether you would be more effective influencing via one-on-one meetings with individual key stakeholders or in a group of all the stakeholders. Knowing your clients' styles can help you anticipate when you may have some hurdles to overcome so that you can prepare a creative compromise in advance, if necessary. The key for Frank is to walk away from the situation with no party feeling they did not get what they wanted. If your client says to you, "I want A," yet based on your expertise you believe that B is the better path to take, you never want the client walking away saying, "I went to HR wanting A and I didn't get A." You want them walking away saying, "I went to HR wanting A but got B instead." The goal is to win them over to plan B. That is how listening, understanding, and learning what works best with your own style and that of your client will assist in exerting impeccable influence.

Another way to look at this is through the lens of Julie, a senior HR vice president at a Fortune 500 information technology company. Her rule for exerting impeccable influence is to align herself with the success, drive and ego of the executive, leader or client she is trying to influence. It may sound a bit insensitive, but it works. Find out what is driving that individual and be there to support what is driving them. Do not talk about the HR initiatives but instead talk about the way you and your team can help their business drivers. The fact is that powerful leaders have egos, and in order to influence them you need to tap into what is driving them and what they need to be successful. This refers back to speaking in their language and repeating what they say so they know that they are heard. If you speak about what is important to them and how your team can back them, it is not about an HR initiative but about how they can reach their objectives. That is powerful and impeccable influence.

Another way to influence is to demonstrate that you can be trusted. For example, Caroline, an HR vice president in a large retail company, had been privy to some confidential information about her vice president of sales and how his behavior and a bad decision caused him to lose a large piece of business. It also damaged the company's reputation in one specific customer segment. When presented with a similar circumstance and under pressure to meet sales numbers, that same vice president started heading in a similar bad direction. In a very subtle and confidential manner, Caroline made one simple comment that was enough to influence him to change directions. Because he trusted her, he knew she was a big supporter of his and was looking out for his best interests, as well as that of the team and the company. Therefore it did not take much effort for Caroline to influence him to do the right thing. Impeccable influence comes much more easily when you have built a trusting relationship with your clients and they know that your influence and recommendations are worthy of their attention.

By using these influencing techniques effectively, HR professionals can influence key business decisions, which adds greatly to being viewed as trusted advisors. A great example of how an HR professional influenced a key business decision comes from a midsized manufacturing company where business conditions were suffering due to poor economic conditions. Layoffs were happening and the business needed to find a way to keep the current workforce motivated and engaged so that they could continue flawless production of their products. The HR director, Rebecca, who supported the operations department in this company, had experience working with high-performance self-directed work teams from a prior role in another company. She knew that in the right environment this type of team structure could be a very effective and motivating way to keep a workforce engaged.

Rebecca spent a great deal of time listening to the concerns of the plant manager and the operations director to get a full understanding of the end result they hoped to achieve with their smaller workforce. She had already built up a solid relationship with these individuals and felt confident that she would be able to approach them with the idea of implementing high-performance self-directed teams in their workforce. Rebecca knew that the clients she supported would want data from similar organizations on the success rate of these types of teams, so she did the research and acquired the information, and she also had her own prior experience to add to her data.

Knowing her own style was more suited to influence one-on-one, Rebecca first approached the plant manager with her idea and shared her data with him. Not only did this begin their brainstorming about how to most effectively go about creating a high-performance self-directed team culture, but he also gave her some other ideas about additional information to gather and share with the senior leaders in the department. Continuing on her "climate-setting" path, Rebecca met one-on-one with each of the key stakeholders about the idea. At the next leadership staff meeting at which they were all together, she presented the final concept and implementation plan for the group to review and approve. By the time she got in front of them as a group, she already had most of their support and buy-in. She had also added each of their suggestions to the final plan for implementation so that when they reviewed it as a group, it was much more comprehensive than in each of the individual meetings.

This is a fantastic example of impeccable influencing that impacted a key business objective. Not only did Rebecca further deepen her relationships with her clients but she also built upon her credibility and demonstrated how critical she was to that organization's success. Rebecca had worked the first two Bridge Principles actively. She had built her base and continued to do things to strengthen that core foundation. Rebecca consistently responded to her clients in a responsible and respectful manner and this enhanced her ability to influence impeccably. She was confident enough to know when she had the right solution to a critical business issue. Based on her own style, she was self-aware enough to know how to best approach her leaders with that solution. She was also confident in her approach because she knew the styles of the leaders and how to make them feel comfortable about implementing such a large-scale culture change. She was courageous and committed enough to go forth with her ideas, work with the business leaders to get the best solution, and drive the solution to closure.

In fact, the self-directed teams, which were implemented several years ago, are still in existence today. The teams consist of non-exempt employees, and are led by a non-exempt employee who is designated a "team lead". Team leads run the teams for a term of two years and then new team leads are nominated and selected by the team members. The company has been able to sustain the current workforce and has not had to lay off any more employees. Their turnover has been minimal and their production rates, quality and customer satisfaction have all increased since the implementation of the teams. And, yes, all this resulted from a program that was developed and implemented by a trusted HR advisor who knew her value and was able to demonstrate it to her clients.

Another example of influencing comes in the form of inserting oneself into delicate situations. Oftentimes business leaders do not realize that they need their HR partner sitting at the table with them while they make key business decisions. It is up to the trusted advisor to be aware of what is going on in the business and to know how and when to insert themselves into these critical situations.

Betty, an HR director with a large consulting company, knew that her company was considering expanding into a new market area that was not part of their traditional core skill set. She had not been involved in the discussions or meetings regarding the specifics of the business expansion, yet had heard enough grumblings about it from employees to know that it was a significant change to the business model under which they currently operated. As someone who had a very solid relationship with the vice president of marketing (who was at the forefront of this market expansion), Betty decided it was time to insert herself into the situation to get more information. Because she had built her base and consistently strengthened it through active relationship-building and responding responsibly to her clients, Betty already had the respect of her clients and, in particular, that of the vice president of marketing. Asking questions of these leaders about business situations was not unusual for Betty, nor was it something they resisted.

As she posed questions to the vice president of marketing, she discovered that expanding into this new area would require a set of skills that the current workforce did not possess. Ironically enough, the vice president of marketing had not even thought about whether or not the current workforce was tooled with the necessary skills to operate in this new area and under a different model. What Betty's involvement did was make the leaders aware of a critical need (people and skills) that had to be filled if the business could be successful in this new area. Since Betty's involvement and recommendation altered the timing of the expansion into this new market, it could have been perceived as a roadblock – but it wasn't. Why? Because Betty had built up her credibility with this group and because she presented her recommendation, not as a required HR need or program, but as an essential ingredient for business success.

Betty noted to her clients that it could be detrimental to the new initiative if they proceeded with the original plan and the workforce was not prepared. Her recommendation was that they get a segment of the workforce prepared and skilled to perform so that when their efforts were successful, they were ready to proceed and serve their new client immediately. She did not direct them or tell them what to do, but instead she presented them with options in addition to her recommendation. The result was that they took her recommendation about how to approach expansion into the new market.

That is a great example of how leaders heeded the advice of their HR professional because they trusted her and knew that she had the business's best interests at heart.

This next example shows what can happen when HR does not influence impeccably and the business leaders do not heed the advice of their HR partner. It comes from a large government contracting company that was going through the due diligence process prior to acquiring another company. HR had been involved in the due diligence process, yet had been excluded from the final decision-making meetings. Patricia was the HR director in this particular division of the company and, unfortunately, was not a respected member of the team. She had not been in her position for very long, and in her short time there had not done the appropriate things to build solid relationships with her clients. Patricia had transferred to the team from another position within the company. She acted in a very parental and controlling way, which turned off her clients and caused them to do what they could to avoid her. This is a clear example of someone who, during the "check your attitude" process, should have realized that she was not suited for this type of HR role. She did not have any desire to be a partner to her leaders, but instead preferred to only be their conscience. She typically told them what they could or could not do in a very parental manner.

In this situation, Patricia's involvement in the due diligence process revealed to her that there was not a good cultural fit for these two companies to merge. Based on some of the glaring cultural differences and some of the employment practices that this new company had engaged in, Patricia's recommendation (which represented the HR recommendation) was to not proceed with the acquisition. Acquiring this company would cost a great deal of unnecessary time and money correcting existing problems in the new company and shifting their culture towards processes currently in practice at Patricia's company. However, because Patricia was not involved in the final decision-making meetings, she needed to insert herself into that part of the process and provide her recommendation. When she did invite herself to a meeting and share the recommendation, it was heard and received with, "Thank you. We will take that into consideration." Because Patricia had not built up her credibility and did not have the respect of the leaders on that team, they dismissed her recommendation as another area in which she was trying to tell them what to do.

The result of this situation was not positive. The new company was acquired, and as Patricia had indicated, the cultural mismatch between the two companies became a liability. Not only did it cost significant time and money to undo many of the unethical processes that the newly acquired company had become acclimated to in the past, but a merging of the two cultures never really occurred. Many of the highly skilled people from the newly acquired company, who were the primary reason for the acquisition, ended up leaving the organization. Clearly, Patricia's advice should have been heeded. But because she did not have the trust and respect of the business leaders in the organization, she was unable to exert any influence on them.

As indicated by these examples, influencing and inserting yourself are delicate skills and you can only be successful if you have the right mindset and behave in a way that puts the best interests of your clients and the company first. HR professionals certainly cannot and should not influence everything that goes on in a business. Not only do you not have that kind of time, but if you try to exert your influence on everything, it will lose some of its impact and not be viewed as valuable. You should choose your influencing opportunities with discretion and focus on areas in which it is required and will mean the most to your business. That is what the next part of impeccable influence is about: focus.

CHAPTER 6

FOCUS

FOCUS IS THE MAJOR FACTOR IN EXERTING IMPECCABLE influence. You should know where to focus your energy and place your influence so that it is meaningful and has impact. In order to do this, you should go back to understanding your clients' objectives and top priorities. The general rule that has been successful for many trusted HR advisors is to know the top three priorities of your business and then work to exert appropriate influence in those areas. By doing this, you will not only get the appropriate attention from your clients, but you will have meaningful impact. Simply base your top three HR priorities on those of the business. If you already do this, then the next few pages might be a refresher for you. But if you are not quite sure, then take this opportunity to find out.

In order to know where and when to exert appropriate influence and to be sure it is impeccable, have a conversation with the top leader in the organization you support and find out the top three business priorities. This is an occasion when you can build credibility as a trusted HR advisor, and it is an opportunity to work on solidifying or re-establishing the relationship. Remember, even if you have mastered Principle I and have a very strong foundational relationship with your clients, it never hurts to do things such as this to remind them of your commitment to their success. In fact, it always helps.

In smaller companies, business leaders don't always dedicate time to working through their strategic priorities or providing this information to HR. These tasks are sometimes accomplished in an impromptu fashion or on an as-needed basis depending upon the type of business, the size of business and the resources available. This is a great opportunity for HR practitioners to exert their influence and not only become part of that process but ensure that all the right players are involved. You can actually facilitate this discussion or facilitate the meeting that drives the business leaders to develop their top priorities and commit them to writing. Then you can mirror your top three priorities after the business's priorities and know exactly which HR programs can and will have the most influence on the success of the business.

In many large corporations, identifying strategic priorities is part of the steady annual business rhythm. If you are not sure what the top strategic priorities are, it might be as simple as asking. Then you can work with your HR team to develop the HR priorities that will support and have direct influence on the success of the business. This is the human resource organization's opportunity to exert focused impeccable influence. It cannot be done without understanding the business objectives and focusing on how HR can align themselves and their objectives accordingly. There are two examples that highlight this concept. One demonstrates what an unfocused HR department looks like and the other demonstrates what a focused HR department looks like.

Imagine you were working in the HR department of a

100,000-person corporation. You were in a new role as the employee development director, and your boss, Phil, the vice president of organizational development, assigned you a new project. The project was to work with internal business leaders and external consultants to develop a competency model for use across the entire non-leader exempt employee population. This was a very large project that would clearly take a lot of time and resources and have a lot of exposure. It came up unexpectedly and it was not something that you and Phil had discussed as part of your objectives for the coming year, but you were told that the senior leaders in HR felt it was something the workforce needed. In February you were told to have the model ready to implement by the end of the year. It would take your time away from a number of your other high-priority projects, but you were excited about working on such a large and complex new project. You saluted and you began.

Fast-forward six months. You spent the past six months and countless hours with external consultants (paid them lots of money), developed the competencies, and occupied the time of a large number of leaders and employees across the corporation to validate these competencies. You ensured they were the best ones to use to assess employees' performance and make hiring decisions. You had kept your boss Phil up to date on the progress and were on schedule with your implementation and communication plan. Believing all along that the senior HR leadership team was up to speed on the progress, you were prepared to brief them on the status of the implementation schedule. You had briefed this same team earlier in the year on your path forward, and you had involved numerous other HR employees and leaders from across the corporation in your project team since becoming the leader for this task. It truly had been a cross-company effort.

You now enter the meeting to update the senior HR leaders on your progress and the next steps. Most of them are in support and excited about your progress. There are a handful who are concerned about the time and resources that will be required for implementation in the coming eight weeks as budgets are tight, and taking leaders and employees away from their everyday tasks to attend training on the competencies might create some issues. Finally, one senior HR leader (who is new to the team) poses the following question to his peers: "How many of you have implementation of this competency model in your objectives for this year?" There is dead silence around the table. He asks a follow-up question: "How many of the business leaders you support have this in THEIR objectives for this year? Do they know that they will be accountable for ensuring all their employees comprehend this and implement it by the end of this year?" Again, silence.

You might be able to figure out the rest of this story. The project was tabled. It was put on hold indefinitely. The months and months of extensive time and resources were also indefinitely postponed so that the senior HR leaders could first go to the presidents and vice presidents of their respective businesses and find out if this was really a need for the entire corporation. They had to find out if the leaders were willing to endorse it and if it was something that would support their business strategy and objectives. This should have been taken care of long before you began work on the task.

The direction that came from Phil was something that most HR professionals have experienced. He had been in a discussion with his boss and two other senior vice presidents during which it came up that it would be helpful if the exempt, non-leader employee population had a competency model to use for their assessment and development. There was already a leadership competency model in place and the discussion was about how successful the leadership model had been and that the same type of framework was needed for the rest of the employee population. Phil took this discussion as a call for action when, in reality, it was a theoretical discussion for further exploration. Phil then asked you to work on this and the rest of the story played out as written above. Again, many HR professionals have fallen prey to this type of situation. You felt excited and ambitious about creating a fantastic program that was actually the idea of one of your superiors, and you charged ahead without remembering the rule of focus.

By using the rule of focus to influence superiors, this situation could look drastically different. Imagine you are now in the role of Phil. You are in a meeting with your boss and two other senior vice presidents. The conversation is about several of the currently successful employee and leadership development programs that have been implemented over the past several years. One of these programs is the leadership competency model that is getting kudos from the company's senior executives. Since this is a program that you led for the entire corporation, you feel a lot of pride in the successful outcome and how well it has been received and engrained into the company culture. Now your boss makes the following comment: "Why don't we work on getting something like that designed for the rest of the exempt population?" to which the other two senior vice presidents resound with, "Yes! That would be great!" Keeping in mind that you are all at corporate headquarters and you are leading a centralized corporate function, you want to immediately consider how this type of large scale program and implementation effort will impact the businesses in the field. Your most appropriate response would be as follows: "Yes, that sounds like a great idea. What I'd like to do is discuss this with my colleagues out in the field and determine how this will fit into their overall plan and objectives for the year." Perhaps you might get some resistance, because if it is something that your boss wants to get implemented, he might push you to just "Get it done." However, you can use your influence skills to listen, understand, and then respond with more information. Perhaps you tell him that the reason the leadership competency model has been such a great success is due to the strong support from the business leaders and that same type of support is required for this type of program, so you need to ensure that there will be this same level of support before embarking on such a large task. Then, go out and gather the data you need from your counterparts in the field to determine the best path forward. Find out what their business strategies and objectives are for this year and whether or not this type of program will support those efforts. If not this year, can it work next year? Is it even needed? Gather all the necessary data to show that it does indeed support the business objectives before charging off and starting the task. And if it is something that does not support business objectives, does not have the support of the business leaders, or will not drive the required results, then that should be all the reasoning you need (with detailed factual data as to why not) to ensure that your superiors respect and support your decision to hold off on such a large scale effort.

As a trusted HR advisor, it is your responsibility to ensure that the HR programs you take responsibility for are in support of your businesses objectives, that they are focused, crisp, and deliver the necessary results. Creating a program that does not have business leader support and, even worse, is simply a directive from the corporate headquarters office, will not help your influence skills nor will it gain you status as a trusted advisor.

Your clients expect you to provide business reasons why certain HR programs must be implemented and why others should not. In this particular example, the competency model ended up being delayed for approximately one year prior to being executed. The effort and work was not lost, but there was certainly some lost momentum as well as lost motivation among the many employees who were involved in the initial "Hurry up and get it done" project. The business leaders agreed that implementing this model would ultimately support their business objectives. However, they needed to work it into their plans, understand it, and make it part of their strategy and path forward as opposed to implementing it just because HR created it (without all of the relevant data).

Remember the rule of focus. It enables you to exert influence. Demonstrating that HR programs are focused and targeted on business results will ease your path to influence the leaders to support them. If they are not focused and targeted, they will not be well received or respected, and it will reflect back on you as the HR advisor.

In an ideal world, in order to avoid the "Phil" scenario described above, HR program ideas would be developed alongside the business goals and objectives. The process is slightly different depending on the size of the company. In a large company, the ideal process works in the following manner: The most senior HR leaders, who are in direct contact with and support the business executives, are part of the business strategy discussions. They provide input into what the key business objectives will be in their particular division of the corporation for a given year. They then propose two or three high level HR initiatives that will support that particular division's objectives.

For this example, assume that there are four of these senior HR leaders for four different company divisions. After their objective-setting meetings for their specific divisions, they get together with their functional HR counterparts (for instance, the senior HR leaders of diversity, compensation, talent acquisition and learning and development). All of the senior HR leaders present the top business objectives for their division and the top HR initiatives that they need in place to support those business objectives. It is then up to this senior HR team (all of the divisional HR leaders and the functional HR leaders), as a whole, to determine which three-to-five HR programs will be developed and executed across the entire corporation. These will be in support of the key enterprise-wide business objectives. They then become the top HR strategic priorities and objectives to be implemented across the corporation in a given year.

The example of the competency model above, when you were Phil, demonstrates how this type of focused objective-setting should occur. In order to have been something that the entire company would have implemented as a new program, the competency model development would have needed to be one of the HR initiatives decided upon as necessary to support one of the top business priorities. This does not mean that new ideas and initiatives will not come up mid-year or outside of this cycle. They will, and they need to be addressed separately. What this does mean is that there is a built-in process or business rhythm that demonstrates how each HR program is in support of and aligned with the overall business objectives. It means that the major HR programs and the resources required for their success are decided upon as part of the development of the business strategy and objectives. This ensures that the company's senior leaders are aware of the programs and in support of them.

Typically there are smaller HR initiatives and programs that occur within a particular business unit or segment of the company that support a specific (smaller) business need. These are the ones, as mentioned above, that are likely to arise outside the broader cycle. HR professionals need to be flexible and able to work within those situations as well. However, large enterprise-wide programs that are not planned for ahead of time are those that tend to create unnecessary stress and turmoil in larger organizations. These are the programs (as in the first scenario for Phil's competency model) that give HR the reputation of being unorganized and not understanding what the business needs to succeed.

If we look at this process through the lens of a smaller company, there might not be as much cross-company coordination needed to determine the top HR initiatives that are required to support the business objectives. The process would be similar in that the top HR leader in the company would meet with senior business leaders to understand the business objectives for the year and provide input on the key HR programs that will support them. Depending on the size of the HR department, this might be the only meeting necessary, or there might be another meeting with the functional HR leaders or the entire HR team to begin to develop the required HR programs. In smaller companies, there is likely more flexibility for developing additional programs that are required or making alterations as needed, however, the rule of focus does not change. The HR programs should be focused on and aligned with the top business objectives, and there should always be the direct link between what HR is doing and the business objectives.

Let's recap the first two Bridge Principles and how they support influencing impeccably. Principle I, Build Your Base, sets the tone and allows you move forward with trust and credibility. Principle II, Respond Responsibly, furthers your credibility as you continue to strengthen the base of your relationships, and sets a positive, engaging tone with your clients. They begin to know what to expect from you as their trusted advisor. Then, when you practice Principle III, Influence Impeccably, you have the credibility to be able to succeed in your endeavors.

It is influencing with focus that is the next stage in establishing even more credibility and which enables you to gain even more trust from your clients. Although these principles support and sometimes build upon each other, keep in mind that this is not a linear model.

These principles and the concepts behind them are strategies that you should keep going back to and refreshing as necessary. They are practices that must be consistently exercised. It is not as if you build your base and then never again take the steps to strengthen your foundation. You should consistently go back and check in on your foundation, ensure your relationships are solid, and then reaffirm or re-establish, as necessary.

Responding responsibly and influencing impeccably are continual and consistent activities. These are the practices and behaviors that you should utilize all the time. Again, if you are not being thoughtful about your responses, then there is little chance of impactful or impeccable influence. That is how these principles build off of each other in a nonlinear way. It is a fluid model that requires movement through and between each principle.

To conclude this topic of impeccable influence, keep it simple by remembering to first be sure you have credibility and respect as you try to exert your influence, and second, make sure your influence is focused on the areas that are most important to your business leaders and to the business as a whole. This is where you can have the most impact and where your impeccable influence skills will help you succeed as a trusted advisor.

APPLY THIS

Influence Skills Checklist

Replay the last critical conversation you had with one of your clients during which you needed to influence them. Can you remember it? (If not, you may need to listen more closely next time!) Think of using these simple steps when you have the same type of conversation again:

- Listen closely. Remember that you are a strong, positive influencer.
- Repeat what you hear back to them in their language.
- Ask yourself, "What would I do or want to do if I were standing in their shoes?"
- Listen to yourself. Check your gut and use your intuition to determine the best recommendation to make to them.
- Link your recommendation to a specific, focused business need or objective.
- Make your suggestion only after going through the above steps.

Checklist available for download at:
www.trustedadvisorreaderspage.com

The "Top Three" Questions

Use these questions when you are working with your clients and your HR colleagues on establishing your top three priorities and the necessary HR programs to support them:

- What are the top three things our business needs to accomplish in the next twelve months?
- What are we doing in HR to support those?
- What are the HR team's top three priorities in the next twelve months?
- Do these top three HR priorities match what we have planned to do to support the business priorities? If not, what can we do to change our focus and ensure that what we are doing in HR directly supports the business goals?

The goal of this exercise is that the top three HR priorities should map directly to the top three business priorities.

Questions available for download at:
www.trustedadvisorreaderspage.com

AUTHOR'S NOTE:
PRINCIPLE III

One of my clients is an HR vice president who was hired into a large organization to be groomed for the position of senior HR vice president. As his "transition" coach, one concept that I focused on with him was impeccable influence. This was where he had the most difficulty as he transitioned into his new role. Because he was highly experienced and ambitious, he wanted to make a good impression and produce results quickly. However, he was not doing a great job of effectively influencing his peers. Others perceived him as entering the organization like a "bull in a china shop" and pushing his agenda forcefully without a full understanding of or appreciation for the culture of his new company. The company leaders did not react quickly to change and needed much more climate-setting prior to adopting new ideas. We worked on getting him to implement some of the influencing concepts discussed in Principle III of the Bridge Model.

This was a starting point for him since he wanted and needed to influence his peers about some of his new ideas.

To more effectively do this, he began using the basic influencing skills of having a picture in his mind of his desired end result, listening closely to his peers as they expressed their input, repeating back to them exactly what he heard, and then listening to his own gut prior to continuing down the path of influencing and making recommendations. Because he was a fast mover with a type A personality, taking the time to do all of this was not an easy shift. It took practice and some focused coaching for him to feel comfortable pausing to listen to others and pausing again to listen to himself so that he could assimilate all the necessary information required to begin to exert his influence more appropriately. He has made some great improvements in this area with these simple, yet impactful actions. Others are beginning to view him as more collaborative and definitely more influential, and that is exactly what we were hoping to achieve.

DISTINGUISH YOURSELF

What does it mean to distinguish yourself? It means to stand out as different and distinct – to have an indicator or an attribute that sets you apart from others. Distinguishers are typically associated with positive characteristics; however, negative characteristics can also set people apart from others. What Principle IV refers to is, in a sense, both. It is about what to do to distinguish yourself as a true trusted advisor and what not to do (things that will single you out as a gatekeeper).

CHAPTER 7

DO

THE MAJORITY OF THIS BOOK DEALS WITH ATTITUDES behaviors and practices that you do want to possess to be a trusted HR advisor. This chapter focuses on the most critical of the "dos". If you cannot do anything else, be sure you do what's in this chapter. That is not to say that the other principles are not critical, but when you are struggling or questioning or are uncertain about what steps to take or how to act or behave, come back to this chapter; it will make all the difference in your being a distinguished, trusted HR advisor. These are the things that trusted advisors do without fail, every time. You will notice some references back to the earlier principles, which further demonstrates the nonlinear structure of this model. There is a need to go back and forth between principles and concepts to be sure you are always acting as a trusted advisor.

The first distinguishing "do" is to be honest and act with integrity. Yes, most people learned this a long time ago, but it still holds true that honesty is always the best policy. Do what you say and say what you'll do. Acting with integrity goes back to what was discussed in

Principle I, Build Your Base. You should be authentic and true to yourself so that you can act with honesty and integrity. Most people can see through falsities and know when someone is not acting with integrity. When this happens it is not only very difficult to regain others' trust but also has a negative impact on the individual's feelings about themselves. It is about being aligned with your true self. The following is an example of an HR leader who was not true to herself. Not only did it have an impact on her job performance, but it had physical manifestations as well.

Jeanne was a senior HR leader who worked in corporate America for over fifteen years and had a successful, fast-moving career. She worked her way up the ranks in a very large company and always played the role of good corporate citizen. She put the company first, took any and all assignments that were given to her, moved around to different geographical locations, and was highly rewarded and compensated for her efforts. She was promoted to an intensely stressful senior level position, and then some things happened in her personal life that made her question her choices and how she was living her life. She went through a year-long soul-searching process and realized that continuing in the current corporate environment at the hectic pace she had been keeping was not something she wanted to do any longer. It had worked incredibly well for her for many years, but she had turned a corner and wanted a different life and lifestyle. She made the decision to leave the company and go out on her own to start her own business about eight months before she actually left. Those eight months before she left were extremely stressful for her because she knew that she was going to leave as soon as she worked through her transition plan, and until that happened, she still needed to be present and engaged at her place of employment and act as if she was still motivated and driven.

Jeanne did not know how to work in that high-paced corporate environment without running at 200 miles-per-hour. Yet running at 200 miles-per-hour when her heart was no longer in it put her at odds with her authentic self. Jeanne spent the better part of the eight months being "out of integrity" with herself. Although her work never suffered outwardly, she suffered a great deal internally, and experienced stomach ailments, heart palpitations and consistent shortness of breath – all as a result of the pressure she was experiencing to perform and act in a manner that was not true to who she was. Although her clients, colleagues and superiors did not notice any performance issues, Jeanne noticed that some of her behaviors did not make her proud. She had little patience for the issues she was presented with, little patience for the team that reported directly to her, and no tolerance for the ever-shifting priorities that came her way.

Although no one ever became aware of any changes in Jeanne, she would not have been surprised to learn that the people she worked with perceived the shift in her behavior and attitude. Once she had given notice that she was leaving (which was met with great sadness yet resounding support and encouragement for her pursuit of her dreams), her physical symptoms subsided and her patience for what she had to deal with increased, and it was all because she did not have to pretend any longer.

Had this situation carried on any longer, chances are there would have been more outwardly noticeable signs of Jeanne's declining desire to be with the company and her performance would likely have become an issue. Ultimately, acting in ways that are not true to yourself will impact you in some fashion. You will not be able to be a trusted advisor if you are not honest, authentic and unable to act in alignment with your true self.

Being honest often requires you to share information or data with your clients which may not be what they want to hear. However, as a trusted advisor, this is an essential "do". You should tell it like it is, and it will earn you tremendous credibility to do so. A great example of this is about Mike, an HR business partner in a Fortune 100 information technology company who worked with Joyce, a vice president in his company, for about two years. Though Mike was in a junior position, he had built up his trusted advisor status with the leaders he supported by using many of the Bridge Principles throughout his young career. After he moved out of this particular role, he kept in contact with many of the leaders he had supported and kept up a close relationship with Joyce in particular.

A few years later, he heard less-than-positive feedback about Joyce from various sources. He heard that she had become extremely difficult to work with and was berating employees unnecessarily and creating a very difficult work environment for her team. Because of Joyce's high-level role (she had since been promoted to senior vice president), no one felt comfortable talking to her about the behavior. As a trusted HR advisor, Mike knew that he needed to say something to Joyce about the perceived behavior. Mike truly cared about her and her success, and also knew the chances were good that she was not aware of how her behavior was impacting the team. How would she ever know if no one told her? If it got bad enough, she could possibly be reported to the ethics department, so Mike knew he had to try his best to intervene before the situation escalated.

Mike met with Joyce and provided her with the feedback he had been hearing. Since they were no longer working at the same office, he had to drive an hour to meet with her. Mike did not sugar-coat anything, but told it like he heard it. He told her that he had received feedback about her behavior that was not good and he wanted to see if she was aware of it. Joyce had not heard any of the feedback prior to Mike's visit. His information was received well because of the relationship he had built with Joyce over the years. By going out of his way to provide her with information that, if not addressed, could have harmed her career, it increased his credibility with her even further. He did not go there to tell Joyce to do anything specific; he went there to share data with her and let her know the potential consequences for her career if she did not make an effort to change these perceptions. Because Mike acted from an authentic and genuine place and not from a place of "I have to do this," or "I should do this," it was very well received. He kept in mind all the Bridge Principles as he spoke with Joyce. He acted authentically, listened well, and tried to understand her point of view. He did not react, remained neutral, and influenced her by placing himself in her shoes. He knew that advancing to the highest ranks in the company was a huge driver for Joyce. He influenced her by telling her, frankly, that if she did not address this behavior, advancing her career to the highest senior level could be in jeopardy.

What Joyce did after Mike met with her and whether she chose to change her behavior or ignore him was her own decision, but what Mike did distinguished him as a trusted advisor. He had the courage to confront a somewhat difficult, high-level individual with information that she might have rejected. He cared enough about this individual and about how she was perceived to do the right thing. That distinguished him not only to Joyce, but also among many other people and, as will be demonstrated in a later example, kept Mike on a very short list of trusted HR advisors.

Another distinguisher is to implement a thought shift from "No" to "How?" HR professionals are often so overwhelmed with work that an easy way to keep things from piling up on their plate is to simply say "No." "No" removes possibility and eliminates excess work. "No" is a response that trusted advisors sometimes do have to give, yet is always one that should be carefully thought through. The best way to do this is to shift your thinking. Each time you want to answer with a quick "No" or you are internally saying, "That is impossible," start thinking, "How can we make this work?" instead. "How?" will often turn into "No" because "No" is often the right answer, but there should always be a "How?" thought process before a "No."

For example, Dave, a senior HR leader for a division of a large retail company, was working with his clients on an affordability challenge. They needed to reduce millions of dollars in costs for the following year, and part of that cutback was going to come in the form of headcount reduction. As with many organizations, this company had an involuntary layoff moratorium during the holiday season so that no one would be laid off between Thanksgiving and New Year's. What this meant was that layoff notices had to go out at least two weeks before Thanksgiving. Two weeks before the cutoff date, the senior vice president and CFO of the division told Dave that they needed to lay off 60 people because they needed at least that many heads off payroll by the end of the year. Dave knew that ranking and selecting 60 individuals for layoff from a workforce of 6,000 would take a lot longer than two weeks. There would need to be significant structure and discipline around the selection process as well as senior level HR and legal review. Realistically it would be nearly impossible to reach this goal considering the constrained timeline.

The easy answer in this situation would have been for Dave to say "No" and, of course, explain the reasons why this objective could not be reached. Considering the time constraints, there would have been little his clients could do to dispute his rationale and they would have had to wait until early in the following year to conduct the layoffs. However, he also knew the seriousness of the cost challenges that his clients were facing, and was committed to helping them reach a solution. So Dave began to think, "How?" How could they eliminate these costs before the end of the year within the guidelines and parameters that they were facing?

After numerous conversations over a very short two-day period, they decided (and got approved by the company's senior leadership) that they would offer a voluntary layoff. This way the cost savings would be realized before year-end instead of in the following year. The result was that over 100 employees volunteered for layoff and were off payroll by the end of that year. There was a lot of planning and coordination that the HR team needed to do to prepare for and execute the voluntary layoff, however this option enabled the division to actually exceed their cost-saving objectives. Because Dave thought "How?" instead of "No," he was able to support his clients in a mutually workable solution. Because he went out of his way to get approval for and execute this task, Dave further distinguished himself as a trusted HR advisor.

Another way to think about this distinguisher is to use a mantra that one of the HR directors interviewed for this book has used throughout her career: "Find a pathway to yes." Of course, there is a balance to this because sometimes "Yes" is not the right answer. HR professionals must often have the guts and courage to say "No." This will be covered in greater detail in Chapter 8, which reviews the distinguishing "don't" characteristics of trusted advisors. (You do not want to be afraid to say "No" when it is the right answer!) However, in the context of the "dos", thinking "How?" or "finding a pathway to yes" is exactly what you should be doing before coming up with the "No." If you apply this thought process and your clients know, without a doubt, that you will work to come up with a reasonable solution, then when you do have to say "No" they will be much more accepting of it. They will know that your response truly must be because "No" is the right answer.

Another great example of this is what one HR executive in a Fortune 100 government contracting company described as "Building up a bank of good will." This is similar to the concept that was just described in that he is consistently going out of his way to figure out the "pathway to yes" whenever it is feasible. This is essentially his "bank of goodwill." When he is unable to "find the pathway to yes," his clients are much more accepting of his "No" because he has already demonstrated that whenever possible he will work as hard as he can to get to the "Yes."

The critical point here is that you have to complete all the due diligence, regardless of what the answer comes out to be. You should work hard to show your clients that you are trying to get to their end result. Sometimes that works and sometimes it does not. You are distinguishing yourself by taking all the necessary steps to determine "how" you can "find the pathway to yes." That distinguishes you as a trusted HR advisor, even if the answer ends up as "No." What will distinguish you as a gatekeeper or roadblock will always be the immediate "No." This refers back to the idea of pausing and not giving an instant response, which was highlighted in Principle II about responding responsibly. It is often the immediate response that results in "No," whereas if you pause or take the "two-hour challenge" to explore other options, you then "find your pathway to yes."

After interviewing many senior-level successful HR leaders for this book, it is clear that one distinguishing "do" characteristic to consistently practice is to seek feedback. Seeking feedback and input from your clients demonstrates that you care what they think of your performance and you have a desire to learn and grow from their feedback. A very easy way to do this is simply to ask your senior leaders one-on-one how you and your HR team are doing. Or you can use the "start/stop/continue" questions, which are: "What should we start doing?" "What should we stop doing?" and, "What should we continue doing?" These three simple questions can provide you with a lot of information and give you a good grasp on where your leaders feel you are adding value and where some things may need to change. When seeking feedback, remember the qualities of responding responsibly. Be open and listen; try not to react or defend against anything that may be counter to what you believe or that may not be what you want to hear. If something you hear upsets you, apply the two-hour rule that was reviewed back in Principle II. Wait at least two hours before responding, or better yet, schedule a follow-up meeting to go over your perceptions of the feedback.

Another way to gather feedback is through a more formalized process. A great example of this comes from a Fortune 500 shipping and transportation company in which each of the senior HR leaders meet annually with their department leaders at the vice president level (and their direct reports) to seek feedback on the performance of the human resources department. These meetings occur across 24 departments and take approximately four to five months to complete. They are invaluable because not only do the HR leaders hear directly how their teams are impacting the business, but this forum also enables HR to share their agenda with the leaders of each department. This ensures that the HR agenda is aligned with the business objectives and that the leaders can adequately support planned HR objectives. This practice is highly valued by HR and the company leaders, and is a great example of how seeking feedback, formally or informally, in a group or one-on-one, can distinguish someone as a trusted advisor.

Another great example provided by Jon, an HR director supporting the CFO of a large government contracting company, is to take risks. This will definitely distinguish you as a trusted HR advisor. The risks, of course, should be calculated ones, and risk-taking is best left until after you have established a solid relationship with your clients in order to ensure the most favorable reception.

Jon began to notice that something seemed off with the CFO; he just didn't seem to be himself. After a few weeks, Jon approached the CFO and asked him if he was okay and if anything was wrong. He explained that he was worried about the CFO due to his atypical behavior over the past several weeks. The CFO was very appreciative of the concern that his HR partner expressed, and was able to share some things that had been going on in his life that were impacting his behavior. The risk taken here was that asking such a personal question could have been perceived as intrusive, but because Jon had established a solid relationship with the CFO, he felt confident that it was the right thing to do. He genuinely cared, was concerned, and wanted to provide an outlet for his client if indeed he was open to talking about it. This kind of risk-taking strengthens relationships and is unquestionably a distinguishing behavior of trusted advisors.

Another crucial "do" that came up as a theme from business leaders is to create boundaries for your clients and keep them as such. Boundaries provide your clients with something to bump up against. A great analogy from one of the HR vice presidents interviewed for this book is to think of crib bumpers that protect babies when they bump up against the edge of the crib and keep them from hurting themselves. For your clients, boundaries are there to remind them that they are getting close to the edge or are up against a potentially uncomfortable or dangerous situation. They remind them that there are legal or procedural limits in place. It is always up to the other person whether or not they cross the boundaries. You cannot control what they do. But your role is to be sure they are aware of the boundaries and to explain to them what it means if they do cross them.

Some other vital "dos" that trusted advisors regularly practice to distinguish themselves include being humanistic, being personable and giving people the benefit of the doubt. These seem like basics, and they are, but unfortunately these simple and basic behaviors often get lost in the shuffle of all the tasks that occupy an HR professional's time. The HR department gets a reputation of designing and redesigning processes and procedures because of a small number of poor performers or bad employees. HR teams often make exceptions and create complexities because of a select few people who create discord among the workforce. This ends up making things more difficult for the majority of the workforce as well as creating suspicion where there may not need to be any. People are generally good and come to work to do a good job. Yes, there are the bad apples, but for the most part they are the exceptions and should not be treated like the rule. Give people the benefit of the doubt. Assume they are telling the truth and treat them like fellow humans.

One senior HR leader at a research company said that what has made her so successful is that she puts "being personal on a personable level" at the forefront of all she does. The fact that this is not a common behavior but a distinguishing behavior is telling in and of itself. It is up to each person reading this to be sure that the trait of being personable is the cornerstone of commonality among the behaviors of HR professionals.

"Some days, it's not about passion and courage. It's not about heroism and drama. Some days, it's not about transcendence or transformation, not about being better than anyone who came before you. Some days, it's simply about delicious acts of doing simple things, simply."

~ ANONYMOUS

CHAPTER 8

DON'T

"The things that you do, which you should not, are often more distinguishing than the things that you do, which you should."

~UNIVERSITY PROFESSOR,
HOFSTRA UNIVERSITY,
HEMPSTEAD, NY

A VERY ASTUTE MAN MADE THAT COMMENT TO A group of college students in the early 1990s. He reminded the group to be wise and remember the things not to do as much as remembering the things to do. This is exactly what this chapter is about – the behaviors and practices that trusted advisors should not do as they continue to distinguish themselves. Another way of looking at this is to remember that the things you should not do, if they happen often enough, continue to keep HR professionals steeped in their gatekeeper status as opposed to elevating them to the status of trusted advisor. This chapter will highlight behaviors, practices, and, unfortunately, many examples of what HR professionals should remember not to do if they want to differentiate themselves as true trusted advisors.

First, HR advisors should not create change and complexity simply for the sake of change. HR professionals often fall prey to creating complex processes and programs and then recreating them because they feel this confirms their value. The more complex the HR process and the more it changes, the greater the need for HR professionals. However, it is human nature to resist change, regardless of how frequently people say they thrive on change. The majority of people are actually uncomfortable with change. In the workforce, change often creates angst and uncertainty. The feeling of "What is coming next?" becomes apparent as people anticipate yet another change in their structure, processes, or programs. Yet because change is constant, that is the way the world operates. Because the human resources department often has to deal with change that comes about from other areas of the company, and has to deal with the workforce reaction to that change, they should keep their self-imposed changes to a minimum. All large-scale HR changes need to be justified with sound business reasoning.

A technology company with 2,500 employees often fell prey to change from the HR department due to the HR team's desire to reach the "next level". They had a new program or an update to an existing program almost every year, and the changes were significant enough to cause consternation in the workforce. For example, they implemented a succession and talent management program that was considered effective and efficient by the business leadership team, yet each year the HR team changed something about the program. The HR team described the changes as "process enhancements," however they were significant enough that the business leaders needed to relearn the system, be introduced to a new set of definitions, or learn a new tool or new terminology. Because the senior leaders felt the existing program was working well, they were not in support of the changes and resisted them.

There was no solid business reasoning behind why this HR team continually tried to improve or enhance a program that their business leaders felt was working. The senior HR leader who shared this information said that she believed she and her HR team fell into the trap of constantly reaching for the next best program and the newest HR trend in an effort to increase their effectiveness and try to add value. However, what they ended up doing was frustrating the company leaders. These failed process enhancements eventually led the HR team to a more simplified and focused change management mindset, and they stopped creating unnecessary change that their business leaders resisted.

Problems also occur when HR creates complex procedures or adds complexities to existing procedures that end up tying business leaders' hands. Barbara, a senior HR leader with another large information technology company, was supporting a division of the company that housed about 10,000 employees. This division had recently gone through a layoff, and several members of Barbara's team were concerned when, within one month of the reduction in force, there were new job requisitions in their staffing system, indicating that they were hiring again. In an effort to make sure that these job requisitions were not for a similar skill set or in the same job family as those of the employees who were just laid off, Barbara inserted herself into the process of reviewing all of the new job requisitions for this division. This was a matrix organization that housed 10,000 engineers for the entire 50,000-person enterprise. The engineers were sent to various company divisions to work on specific programs for specified periods of time, and then when projects or programs ended, they would return to their "home department" and were reassigned to another place in the company where their skills were needed. As new programs were won or new business developed, there was often a need for new skill sets and additional employees. There was typically some level of hiring occurring all the time, since there might be one part of the company that was laying off but another part that was growing and thriving, requiring people and positions with different skill sets.

This particular situation became exceedingly cumbersome and complex due to the decision made by Barbara and her HR team. The decision to have Barbara review all newly-posted job requisitions, regardless of level or job family of the position being filled, added a step to the process. This caused a bottleneck in the flow of staffing new positions. First, Barbara was not always able to review the job requisitions in a timely manner, and second, she typically had more pressing things to do than review all the entry-level positions open for new hires. However, she kept this process in place because she did not trust the leaders' ability to manage their own business and do the right thing.

This is a huge "don't" for trusted advisors. The HR department is not there to monitor or police the way leaders run their businesses; it is there to provide advice and counsel. And, if HR professionals are trusted advisors, the clients they support will typically heed their advice and counsel without such policing. In this situation, Barbara should have provided advice and counsel about which positions should and should not be open and filled on the heels of a layoff. It would then have been up to the leaders to consider this guidance and act accordingly. The HR department did not need to get in the way and monitor everything.

Another distinguishing "don't" is in regard to the topic of consistency. HR departments are frequently known for creating procedures that enforce consistency and fairness in how employees are treated. Policies make it easy to be consistent. Yet what you do not want to do is be consistent simply because it is easier or because it is required by the policy. Policies and procedures should be used as guidelines, not as laws. Yes, there are employment laws that all HR practitioners need to be aware of and provide guidance for, but policies and procedures should not be treated like laws. In speaking with a number of business leaders and HR professionals about some of the behaviors that make HR professionals trusted advisors, a common theme was about being consistent, yet allowing for flexibility.

For example, in a Fortune 500 food products company that has over 30,000 employees, the need for flexibility is as important as the need for consistency. The succession planning process in this company was derived from requirements set forth by the corporate office. The corporate office determined which positions needed to have successors identified for them and what material and information would be included in the annual succession review with the CEO of the company. This information was distributed to all the divisions of the company as the minimum requirement. Unfortunately, many interpreted the data-gathering requirements as strictly set in stone.

In a 5,000-person division of the business, the vice president wanted to go much deeper with the succession planning. She had some critical roles in her division for which she wanted to start developing successors, yet her HR director told her that she could not do that – that the corporate office dictated the only positions for which succession planning was to be done. The HR director indicated that for the sake of consistency in practices across the corporation, she was not permitted to expand on the corporate requirements. This was clearly not the case, but this was the message from the HR director. It created the perception of inflexibility without good reason.

In another division of the business, another executive wanted to do the same thing; he wanted to go deeper and broader in his succession planning. His HR director had the proper understanding that the corporate office requirements were minimum requirements, and were there to promote consistency and not to restrict the company divisions from doing additional succession planning.

In larger companies that encompass many different divisions with different needs, it is essential for HR to be flexible while at the same time being consistent. Trusted HR advisors work with their clients to determine what works best for their business and meet their particular business needs. They do this while working within the constraints of things like "corporate requirements," and they go back to the distinguishing "do" behavior of thinking "How?" instead of "No."

Speaking of saying "No," this reveals the next distinguishing "don't", and that is: Don't be afraid to say "No!" Chapter 7 reviewed why it is important to ask "How?" instead of saying "No." Yet that referred to using "No" as an instant response to remove work from your plate or avoid working with your clients to come up with an appropriate solution to their situation. This is about having enough courage and conviction to say "No" when it is the right answer and having the respect of your clients so that they hear and respect your "No."

For example, an HR director at a non-profit organization is focused with her team on "teaching their managers to fish instead of fishing for them." This often requires saying "No." In this organization, a new process was implemented in which leaders had responsibility for conducting career discussions with all their employees. As well, they had to document various pieces of the discussion in the talent management system. They had to indicate when the discussion occurred, key strengths and developmental opportunities that were discussed, and the employee's next possible assignment. Early on in this process, the managers strongly persuaded their HR partners to enter the data into the system for them, and this is where HR needed to push back and say "No." The managers committed to the process when it was introduced and they took ownership of it. They accepted responsibility for being partners with their employees in career development. In spite of that, they did not want to complete the full cycle of the required elements in the procedure. Having HR professionals take over for the administrative task was not the best use of the HR professionals' time and could have led to issues with the integrity of the data that was entered into the system. If the HR team had to transcribe what actually went on during a discussion at which they were not present and enter that information into a talent management system, errors could be made. And engaging someone from HR at the administrative level would relieve the managers of full ownership of the procedure. This type of situation is one in which HR professionals need to push back, say "No," and hold leaders accountable for the things they need to take ownership of and for which they are responsible.

As trusted advisors, you need to teach and guide leaders to lead and not do things for them ("teach them to fish instead of fishing for them"). The more that HR professionals absolve clients of their duties and take on tasks that clients should be doing themselves, the more HR professionals are classified as "pleasers". What also can happen is that the more HR says "Yes" when they should be saying "No," the more difficult it will be to ever say "No." Additionally, HR professionals should keep appropriate boundaries between themselves and their clients so they do not get too embedded in their clients' issues, which can create conflicts of interest. This assists in remembering that their role is to provide advice and counsel so that their clients can make the best decisions for their organizations. If HR professionals do not keep appropriate boundaries, they can lose sight of the fact that "No" is often the best piece of advice and counsel that they can give. If they cannot say "No" when it is appropriate, they will not gain the respect of their clients as trusted advisors.

Another example of when saying "No" is appropriate is when your clients want to do something that could be detrimental to their organization or particular department. In a Fortune 100 company that had recently merged with another large organization, there were many duplicate roles as well as many employees doing similar jobs who were classified in different job codes. The vice president of a 100-person department within this corporation wanted to reclassify the job codes of approximately ten people on her team. Although this was the right thing to do, reclassifying the ten would have impacted those outside of her small team who also were doing similar work. In this situation, the right thing to do was an overall cross-company look at all the employees in these types of jobs who might be misclassified, then reanalyze all jobs so that everyone was being treated the same. Especially in regard to job classification, which impacts pay, it is vital that all employees within a particular organization are treated similarly. Reclassifying a select ten people could put the company at risk of being perceived as treating people preferentially (especially if pay would be impacted). The right answer for HR to provide in this situation was, "No, reclassifying these select ten is not the right thing to do," and then to further explain why and how it needed to be part of a broader organizational plan to reanalyze the positions of all individuals in that job classification.

There is another aspect of the word no to address as a "don't", and that is not to be afraid to hear the word no. As an HR professional, you likely hear and feel some resistance from your clients regarding the programs and initiatives that you try to implement. If you work through Principle III effectively, know how to focus on what is important to your clients and what programs they need to meet their business objectives, and influence accordingly, then you are already ahead of the game when hearing their resistance or hearing "No." However, you may hear it regardless of whether the program you are implementing is one they supported. This is when you have a great opportunity to strengthen the relationship and use these trusted advisor behaviors and practices.

For example, imagine that one of your focused HR objectives is to implement a new mentoring program for the purpose of increasing knowledge transfer within your organization. When you are ready to kickoff the new program, you hear "No" from your senior leaders. You might want to react and get defensive and remind them that they signed up for this, but don't. One of the trusted HR advisors interviewed for this book said that when she hears this type of response, she listens through the resistance of the "No" response and seeks out what is behind it. This is a great opportunity for HR professionals to, as Steven Covey says, "seek to understand." Ask your clients what the root cause for their "No" is, and address their fears. You might find out that priorities shifted and the leaders cannot take on mentoring relationships at this time, or perhaps a large program or some key part of the business is in jeopardy so resources must be focused elsewhere. Don't be afraid of or resist their "No," but help them work through the reasons why and get to the root cause.

This leads to our next "don't", and that is don't be afraid to ask "Why?" or "Why not?" This feeds directly from the prior example. Don't accept the answers you hear or the resistance you hear at face value. Ask "Why?" or "Why not?" and then work with your clients on a solution that produces the best outcome. By asking "Why?" or "Why not?" in the previous example, the reason behind the resistance will surface and you can formulate an alternate path; perhaps you delay the implementation of the mentoring program or go forward with a small pilot group of leaders who are not impacted by the shifting business priorities. By not accepting "No" at face value and by asking questions such as "Why?" and "Why not?" you show that you are committed to doing what is best for your clients and the business and you continue to gain their respect as a trusted advisor. Remember that they might not necessary like what you are telling them but they will respect you for having the guts and conviction to share information that is in their best interests.

The next "don't" that came out as a solid theme among the many trusted HR advisors and business leaders who contributed to this book is one that really should not be in the list of "don'ts", yet it is. (And, upon reflection about its severity, it probably should be the number one "don't"!) Don't, under any circumstances, gossip or break confidences. A senior leader and trusted HR advisor in a well-known pharmaceutical company said that HR professionals could not be proud of their ability to keep their mouths shut. HR personnel are the keepers of the keys and have access to a lot of sensitive and personal information, yet are also often seen as the gossipers. Many HR professionals break confidences by sharing information that they should not. As you know, sharing confidential information is grounds for termination and gossiping is not, yet it often has similar damaging consequences, if not for the people being spoken about, then most definitely for the HR person who is speaking. Simply stated: Keep your mouth shut. Don't gossip and don't trade stories. This violates the rule that what is told to HR is told in confidence and also violates the general "need to know" rule that all trusted advisors should follow. If there is not a need for someone else to know what you know about another employee or a business issue, then simply don't say anything.

Because of their roles and the data to which they have access, HR professionals should hold themselves to the highest standard in this regard. If you break a confidence, your status as a trusted advisor will be lost. There is no excuse and no reason for it. If you make the mistake of breaking a confidence, accept responsibility for it, be accountable for your actions, and don't blame it on someone else or some circumstance that was beyond your control. Blaming others for their own mistakes was also cited as an example of what HR professionals often do but should not. It is another vital "don't".

There are a few other key "don'ts" to share. First, don't fall into the trap of believing that the HR agenda takes precedence or priority over the business leaders' agenda. Remember that the business is not there to serve HR but HR is there to serve the business. If you have been following the Bridge Principles, you know that the HR agenda must follow and support the business agenda. If you lose sight of this you lose credibility.

For example, referring back to an earlier example about the implementation of a new performance management system in a Fortune 500 transportation and shipping company, this HR team never lost sight of the fact that their implementation of the system was in direct support of, and secondary to, the business objective of having a high-performing workforce. When the HR team rolled out their program, they were flexible with the method and speed with which pieces of the process were adopted and implemented by each of the company divisions. They had an overall schedule to meet, and within that overall schedule they let each division and department do as much as they could do in a given performance cycle. The accomplishments and progress of each division or department were dependent upon what the particular division's or department's agenda and priorities were during that cycle. This clearly demonstrates keeping the business agenda ahead of the HR agenda and remembering that HR is there to support the business and not vice versa.

Another "don't" that came across loud and clear from the book contributors is don't try to be strategic with your clients unless you have demonstrated that you are capable and knowledgeable about the HR basics. If you do not have the tactics of HR mastered, if you do not have your HR house in order and cannot function at the basic level, then you will not have enough credibility to act like the strategic partner. This is where HR competencies, knowledge, skill and education come into play. Demonstrate that you have the proper and basic HR knowledge prior to being strategic; doing things in reverse order will damage your credibility and have a negative impact on your status as a trusted advisor.

Another distinguishing "don't" is to not be parental. Don't try to control your clients or tell them what to do. If we go back to the example of crib bumpers from Chapter 7, remember that you have set the boundaries but your clients are adults who make their own decisions about whether or not they will cross the boundaries. Don't tell them what to do, as a parent would, but instead explain to them the consequences of crossing boundaries and let them make their own decisions. Don't be the controller; be the consultant and advisor.

A great example of a detrimental behavior that HR professionals tend to practice came from an HR vice president at a Fortune 100 information technology company. She said not to be "Concierges HR"; that is, don't wait for someone to call, fill the order and check the box with a big smile. HR professionals are not servants. They serve the business but are not servants of the business. There is a big difference. If you serve the business, you are out in the business working with your clients to understand exactly what they need to reach their objectives. A servant waits to be called on and fills the order. Don't be a servant.

One of the final two "don'ts" which were themes among book contributors was not to be too emotional. This goes back to Principle II, Respond Responsibly. Don't react or emotionally respond to things you hear or that are presented to you. Step away, walk away, take the two-hour challenge, and then reply. Reacting emotionally can harm your credibility and cause your clients to be skeptical about the types of information they can share with you. If you react emotionally, they may assume that will always be your reaction and they may be inclined to share less information with you.

The second of the final two "don'ts" is to not go too fast or too slow, but instead be flexible with your style so that it matches your client and meets their needs. For example, if you are always in a hurry and your client tends to need more time to process things, your speed may cause your client to feel unsettled. Similarly, if you move slowly and your client processes things very quickly, your slower pace may cause them to feel frustrated. You should be flexible enough to go where they want to go at the speed with which they are comfortable. It does not mean that you need to change the genuineness of who you are; it means that when you are interacting with that clients, your primary focus needs to be communicating and interacting with them at a pace at which they will hear, understand and respond.

Some of these "don't" behaviors may seem very basic and elementary, however they are typically the ones that are easily forgotten about because they are so basic and elementary. HR professionals get so caught up in the fast-paced nature of their everyday jobs that they can easily lose sight of the things that are the most fundamental to their profession. Remember the quote at the beginning of the chapter: "The things that you do which you should not are often more distinguishing than the things that you do which you should."

How do you want to distinguish yourself?

APPLY THIS

Dos & Don'ts Checklist

Do:
Be honest.
Act with integrity.
Be true to yourself.
Think "How?" instead of "No."
Find a pathway to "Yes."
Seek feedback.
Be humanistic and personable.
Give others the benefit of the doubt.

Don't:
Create change for the sake of change.
Create complex procedures for the sake of complexity.
Force consistency simply because it is easier.
Be afraid to say "No."

Be afraid to hear "No."

Be afraid to ask "Why?" or "Why not?"

Gossip.

Be strategic before knowing the basics.

Put the HR agenda before the business agenda.

Be too emotional.

Go too fast or too slow.

This checklist is available for download at:

www.trustedadvisorreaderspage.com

When to think "How?" instead of "No."

Use these questions to discern when to think "How?" instead of saying "No."

1. Is the situation or request putting the company at risk for legal reasons? (If yes, the answer could be "No.")

2. Is the situation or request unreasonable within current time or process constraints? (If yes, think "How?")

3. Is the situation or request something that could be worked out over a period of time? (If no, the answer could be "No;" if yes, think "How?")

4. Is this situation or request something that I can resolve with my clients if I put in considerable thought, time and effort? (If yes, think "How?" If no, the answer could be "No.")

Remember to focus on "Finding a pathway to yes," and be brave enough to say "No" when that is the right answer.

These questions are available for download at:
www.trustedadvisorreaderspage.com

———— AUTHOR'S NOTE: ————
PRINCIPLE IV

I conducted group coaching with an HR team that had received third party feedback that they were not being effective in providing HR support to their business leadership team. The third party feedback came from some of the HR team members' peers in other departments. They heard things such as "No one likes dealing with HR," and, "The leaders avoid HR anytime it is possible." They also heard that business leaders were holding what they called "non-HR" meetings and HR would purposefully be left off the meeting invitation list. The senior HR leader of this team knew that she had some performance issues on her team and also knew that she needed to do something to address the way her team was perceived and help them reach a new level of providing outstanding support to the business. As I worked with this group, it became quite easy for them to begin to distinguish themselves as trusted advisors. They simply had to begin to act the part.

First, each member of the HR team was tasked with approaching their most senior business leaders to gather feedback and get their perceptions (first hand) on the performance of HR.

I then worked with the team to consolidate all the information they received and list areas in which they clearly needed development as well as areas of strength for the team. They chose three areas of significant impact in which to work on improving their performance and begin to distinguish themselves as trusted advisors. One was ensuring that the business agenda always came before the HR agenda and that the HR agenda was always in support of the business agenda. Another was to be more flexible while ensuring consistency. The last was to ensure a continuous feedback loop so that the process of gathering feedback from the business leaders was instilled as a regular quarterly occurrence. Each team member committed to these items and there were consequences for not meeting these expectations which were communicated and understood by all. Although these processes may not seem like a big deal, for this HR team they were their distinguishing factors. Because of how they had been perceived and the low opinion the leaders had held of them in the past, making these simple changes began to shift the way the team was viewed by their business leaders.

GET OUT OF THE WAY

Get out of the way? That might sound a bit odd but it really makes perfect sense and is a concept that is quite simple. You are at a point now where you have, hopefully, been practicing each of the first four Bridge Principles consistently; you are moving back and forth between them and are committed to regularly acting as a trusted HR advisor. Now what you need to do is simply have faith; faith that your clients know what to do and when to come to you if they do not know what to do. You need to have faith that you have been focused and have provided them with enough guidance to act. You need to have faith enough to get out of their way so they can do their jobs and, just as important, faith to get out of your own way.

CHAPTER 9

DO LESS
WITH LESS

HUMAN RESOURCES DEPARTMENTS ARE NOTORIOUS for consistently trying to prove their value and do more and more with fewer and fewer resources. HR professionals should be commended for their efforts to try to add value, but as discussed in the chapter about focus, it is important to remember that something is only "value-added" if it supports or propels the business objectives; it is only value-added if your clients are endorsing whatever you are doing. Instead of continuing to do more with less, why not reconsider this concept and instead "Do Less With Less"? It is widely known that budgets typically get cut first in overhead or support departments like HR. The HR department is frequently forced to work with less. Instead of trying to do more with that, why not do less? Why not create fewer initiatives with fewer task teams and utilize a targeted set of resources for these initiatives? These initiatives should be related to the top three priorities that were defined in Chapter 6 about focus. Doing less does not mean that you are contributing less; it means that you are honed in on what is most important to the business and targeting your resources and efforts towards those things. Since you are possibly already performing with fewer resources (people and budget), why not use your people and budget in a very concentrated manner? If you do not, you may fall into the trap of trying to do more with less and being seen as scattered, not having a clue about what you are doing, or, in more serious cases, being viewed as part of a dysfunctional HR department.

For example, there was an HR department in a large information technology company that notoriously equated "number of objectives" with hard work and productivity. In fact, it was not atypical for a senior level HR manager in the company to have as many as twenty objectives in one year. Yes, twenty. It is very difficult to appropriately or efficiently focus on achieving twenty objectives in a single year, however, that was the mindset in this company. In fact, there was also a matrix management structure so that some HR professionals reported to two different leaders: a divisional HR vice president and a central (or functional) HR vice president. Or, they reported to a business leader in the division they supported and also to a corporate HR vice president. It was not unheard of for these HR professionals to have to map their own objectives to twenty or thirty (yes, thirty) that belonged to their "divisional HR or business leader boss", and then try to map them to a separate twenty or thirty that belonged to their "corporate HR boss".

As you can imagine, this created a feeling of chaos. And, as you also can imagine, this feeling of chaos started at the top. The senior vice president of HR rolled out sixty (yes, sixty!) objectives one year. Needless to say, this HR department was not widely respected. Many of the business leaders saw the HR team as mostly ineffective and highly inefficient. They were viewed as "getting in the way of themselves," over-engineering everything, and consistently trying to implement complex HR programs and processes that provided little benefit to the business. Why were they doing it? Because in some way, shape or form these programs and processes aligned to one of those sixty objectives. They felt as if they had to do what they were directed to do and being measured against by their senior vice president of HR. The business leaders had little respect for some of them and little patience for many of the HR initiatives or actions that impacted their business.

Clearly this is an extreme example but, in a situation like this, the HR leadership should do a much better job of creating more distinct objectives in big, medium, and small companies alike. They should create focus for their teams and be the face of clear business priorities for their clients. They need to create simple processes and procedures that support the business and are endorsed by their clients.

A great example of doing less with less is actually in this same company that had sixty HR objectives. After many years of unsuccessfully pushing an exorbitant HR agenda that did not have a clear focus, they began shifting towards more focused priorities and a sharp, clear agenda. They moved from an agenda that created new programs and ideas for no other reason than to have new programs and ideas, to one that created new programs with crisp focus.

This company had a business objective of cross-business and cross-function talent development for the purpose of grooming internal successors for the most senior level positions. Although they currently had a robust talent-planning process, it was somewhat inconsistent across the corporation (which consisted of over 100,000 employees in over 70 countries in 5 different business units). It was also quite cumbersome in that it required gathering a great deal of information that typically was not utilized after it was gathered. The senior HR leaders recognized that it was vital that everyone speak the same language and follow a common process to reach the objective of developing talent that could move from business to business and function to function and be groomed for senior level positions. They also recognized that to be able to do this, the process needed to be crisper and less cumbersome. Hence the task of unburdening the process began.

The task was to design a consistent, high-potential talent management framework that included common language, processes and applications across the enterprise. The group that was tasked with this project was the corporate talent management team. They were located at corporate headquarters and this made them the least qualified to work on such a task. Therefore the first step was to get the field talent planners engaged as a part of the task team. In this company, the talent planners were the HR professionals working with the leaders in their respective businesses to identify high-potential talent. Not only did they know what the current processes were, but also what their specific businesses could handle as far as potential process changes. Hence it was vital to have them involved from the beginning.

For three days, ten people met in a conference room with one objective in mind: Develop a common high-potential talent identification framework that was user-friendly, simple to implement, and would meet the corporation's executive leaders' requirements for the annual talent-planning cycle. The following questions were posed and answered: "Based on the corporate talent-planning requirements, what is each particular business unit currently doing to meet the requirements? What is working well? What needs to be improved?"

Answering those questions showed that the various businesses identified high-potential talent using some of the same parameters, but many more different ones. Most importantly, it enabled the team to come up with a process that would work the best for the enterprise. It also revealed which pieces of the process were currently value-added and used regularly across the enterprise and which were nothing more than cumbersome exercises in gathering data.

What resulted was the identification of the vital pieces of the process that would remain and those that would no longer be considered corporate requirements. This was a big step towards doing less and making the process crisper. The next thing that resulted was common terminology. For example, the process was named "high potential talent identification" as opposed to the variety of names that had been used previously.

Next the group developed a three-part process for identifying the high-potential talent. This three-part process was as follows: First, assess the employee's high-potential status based on using an enterprise-wide, 9-block potential-performance matrix which was already in place. Next, identify the ultimate potential and position that the employee could reach. There were specific talent pools designated for the ultimate-potential positions. These were pools that were specific to the critical talent and leadership positions within this company, such as president, executive vice president, and program director. And, finally, identify the individual's readiness level for that specific position. The company had already defined these readiness levels, for example: "ready now", "ready six months", "ready two years", "ready two-five years", etc.

The application of this process needed to be common across the corporation so the group also determined how these steps would be applied. It was proposed that, at a minimum, all leaders at the director-level and above would be required to assess their employees using this process. Business units had the flexibility to go deeper than that if they chose to but there was a minimum requirement to meet. In addition, the team recommended that talent review meetings be required at the senior leadership level in all business units across the corporation at least twice per year. This would ensure that the high-potential talent assessments were calibrated and that individuals were discussed during these review meetings.

Although it was unknown how well the task team's proposed framework would be received, the senior vice president of human resources and the senior HR leadership team approved all of it.

The next step was to proceed with implementation across the corporation. Implementing this framework was not as difficult as one might have anticipated simply because this company had already been identifying high-potential talent quite regularly for a number of years. However, it was still a change and needed to be handled as such. The annual talent-planning cycle kicked off early each year and it was at that time that this new framework was introduced to the business leaders. As part of the kick-off, educational material was provided which detailed the new high-potential talent identification framework. The new process was well-received by the leaders, but one of the challenges was getting everyone to adopt the new terminology. Some of the new language replaced verbiage that had been in place for many years. Repetition and "gentle correction" was the best way to combat this challenge. Gently reminding leaders of the new terminology and continually repeating the new language eventually resulted in its common usage.

In addition to educating the population, the other key to successful implementation was getting support from the senior leaders of the businesses in promoting the positive aspects of the new framework. For example, when conducting all-employee meetings, leaders included information about the new talent identification framework and the importance of having a consistent cross-business process to identify the talent of the future. This helped to drive the message and engrain it into the culture. The credit for the positive reception of this process and the ease of implementation was attributed to the collaborative way in which the framework was developed. If the field talent planners had not been included, it would not have been as well-received. Because these were the HR professionals who had the ears of the leaders in the businesses, many of the changes in how high-potential employees were identified came directly from the feedback and ideas of the leaders of the businesses. This had direct impact on the ease with which they adopted it.

This updated process has resulted in many benefits. The biggest improvement has been seen via comparison of talent from different business units. Prior to instituting a common language, process and application, there was often disagreement among senior leaders regarding whether someone was or was not truly a high-potential employee. With common language and common processes in place to identify this talent, there was an "apples to apples" comparison of the talent, and leaders were speaking the same language. Therefore, they meant the same thing when they said, "...an executive high-potential who will be ready in two-to-five years for a vice president role." This fed into the second benefit, which was the senior leaders' greater willingness to share talent across the corporation. Previously, leaders were hesitant to give up their high-potential and high performing employees because they were not sure about who they were getting as replacements for those they were letting go on to new assignments in other businesses. With the common framework and the use of talent interchange meetings, there was greater and more consistent dialogue across all businesses regarding the high-potential talent. Leaders had more confidence in the talent they received from other businesses and greater willingness to share and move talent around. This continues to benefit the corporation and the employees.

There was also much greater confidence in differentiating the development of employees who were identified as high-potential. Previously, employees who got nominated to participate in the high-potential employee development programs were not necessarily high-potential or those who would excel in or benefit from those programs. After the process enhancements, the participants were much more likely to be those who would get the most out of this differentiated development. The implementation of the consistent framework also contributed to a much more robust succession planning process. The senior leaders had much better knowledge of the high-potential talent across the enterprise and had a greater amount of confidence in the assessment of the talent. Therefore, they were more likely to have a cross-section of successors identified in their succession plans. Additionally, this process enabled a broader and deeper level of high-potential talent identification. With some minor tweaks to some of the talent pools, it became possible to easily identify the early career high-potential talent as well as the technical high-potential talent across the corporation.

The advantages to taking the time to apply a consistent method of identifying high-potential talent have been many, and that sentiment is felt among both the HR and business leadership population. The only recommendation for improvement was to have done it sooner rather than later. As this company realized, completing this task brought their process much more in line with a dictionary definition of "consistent". It is now marked by regularity and agreement and, in turn, has opened up additional opportunity to deepen, broaden and strengthen the talent-planning and development process.

This example is a great demonstration of doing less with less. The objective was to have a more consistent and efficient process, and the team that worked on it eliminated a number of the cumbersome steps. For instance, prior to the change, leaders were required to manually gather developmental data on employees. But the data they gathered was not vital or even discussed or reviewed because it was deemed as inaccurate due to the manual nature with which it was gathered. Although it was important to have this type of data available, the team recommended a system fix so that it could be entered into and pulled from their talent management system at any time of the year. This eliminated it from the talent identification process. Although leaders still needed to enter talent development data into a system, it would not be part of this particular process and they would not be required to gather it manually; it could be pulled from the system any time it was required. The team also eliminated some of the confusing terminology and focused the talent identification requirements on a specified number of positions and a specified group of people at certain levels. Again, this required less work of the HR team and less work of the business leaders, yet made the process more robust. Doing less actually gave them richer and more useful data.

This example is a great demonstration of the use of the Bridge Principles. You can see where Principles I-IV, and now the first concept of Principle V, come into play.

The involvement from the field talent-planners was where Principle I came into play. These were the HR professionals who had built their base relationships with the business leaders in the field. They were the ears and eyes of the front-line leaders out in the field and they had the trust of their leaders as they participated on this team. They kept that trust by appropriately representing their leaders' thoughts and perceptions about the talent identification process and how they thought it needed to be improved, as well as where it was working well. They also collaborated well, as an HR task team, by responding responsibly (Principle II) to each other. There were definitely some tense moments during their three-day meeting, but through the efforts of a skilled facilitator all group members were able to get their points across clearly and kept their attitudes and body language in check. They all knew that they had the same desired outcome: a less cumbersome, more consistent process. Keeping the end result in mind, they worked diligently to reach that desired goal (Principles I and II).

As you refer to Principle III, Influence Impeccably, keep in mind that each team member was coming from a different perspective. This company has five different businesses, each with slightly different objectives and, in some cases, very different cultures. All team members had to keep these facts in mind as they worked to influence each other. Through the help of their facilitator, they listened to each other closely and tried to get a true understanding of each other's perspectives. Remembering that the Bridge Model is fluid, they repeatedly went back to their desired end state and recalled that they were all part of the same corporation working towards that same overarching goal. This focus assisted them in their impeccable influence.

Keeping Principle IV in mind, regarding the concepts around distinguishing yourself, these team members showed up for three full days as authentic trusted advisors. They were honest with each other, they were open, they acted with integrity, and they kept the commitments they made to their leaders. They also kept the commitments they made to each other as a team. As much as people sometimes wanted to say "No" to suggestions that were made (and perhaps some did), they made every effort to revert to thinking "How?" instead of sticking with "No." They also were extremely aware of how creating change in this process would impact their individual businesses and the corporation as a whole. They were not interested in creating change unless it was focused and made sense as it related back to the original objective: a more consistent, less cumbersome process.

And this brings us back to Principle V, Get Out Of The Way. Because this team successfully developed a more consistent and less burdensome process, not only did they demonstrate the concept of doing less with less but they also enabled themselves to get out of the way. By making it user-friendly and simpler for leaders, and by not creating complex change, they enabled and empowered their leaders to take charge and to own the talent identification process. Of course, the HR department still needs to be there to provide guidance and counsel, but they do not need to be there to supervise or repeatedly explain an over-engineered process. This is what doing less with less does for HR professionals; it eliminates the need for the gatekeeper and brings forth the behaviors of a trusted advisor.

CHAPTER 10
WHAT GETS MEASURED GETS DONE

THE SECOND KEY CONCEPT INVOLVED IN GETTING OUT of the way revolves around measuring performance and holding leaders accountable for the HR actions and programs they have agreed to undertake. This does not mean that you act as the parent or the police officer but that you simply let them run their businesses while actively working the HR initiatives that support their businesses.

How you effectively do this is by deciding exactly what your clients need to accomplish relative to HR programs. Remind them which HR programs support their business objectives and provide them with concise and realistic metrics for which they will be held accountable. Because you have been actively and consistently practicing the first four Bridge Principles, this process should flow smoothly. You have built your base, continued to respond responsibly and behaved in ways that distinguish you as a trusted advisor. Because of this, you are able to influence your clients and collaboratively set measurements with them that support their business objectives. Remembering that the Bridge Model is fluid, you should be moving back and forth between principles, as necessary, and will likely be doing so as you work on this concept of setting measurements so that you can continue to get out of the way.

The measurements you establish with your business leaders cannot be arbitrarily set. They must be precise measurements that will drive the results they need in their business. For example, if the business is in a growth mode and needs to hire 50 new sales professionals in the upcoming twelve months, then holding the leaders accountable for meeting that number (because it will support their business growth) is the standard that they should be measured against. Additionally, there should be consequences for not meeting the established numbers. Depending upon your culture, it might be useful to include the HR metrics for which leaders and employees will be held accountable in performance objectives. That way, performance ratings or bonuses could potentially be impacted if they are not met.

One Fortune 500 healthcare company uses a weighted system for their HR objectives, which enables leaders to get an "adder" to their performance or bonus rating if they exceed the objective. For example, one of the measurements that the leaders are held accountable for in this company is to have career discussions with all employees who are considered high-potential. Meeting this objective keeps the weighted score for that objective at 1.00. If the objective is not met, the weighted score goes down to .95 and if, perhaps, the leader decides to have career discussions with all employees (not just the high-potential employees but all those who report to them), their weighted score would go up to a 1.05. Depending on the level of the leader, this could actually increase the amount of money they receive as a bonus payment, or if they were a lower level leader it would increase their performance rating for the year, which would have direct impact on their merit increase.

As most of you probably have experienced, leaders pay attention to and focus on how they are being measured. Very rarely do they ignore items pertaining to business finances, (such as orders, sales, EBIT or cash). That is because these are standard items that they will be measured against and, if missed, would potentially impact their performance rating and salary. Having leaders (and individual contributor employees, if appropriate) held accountable for and measured on the HR programs and initiatives that they are responsible for gets their attention and causes them to remain engaged and involved. What gets measured gets done, and what you should do, as the trusted HR advisor, is work with your clients to set the appropriate measurements. You then should guide and counsel them to reach the set objectives; not do the work for them or force them to do what they do not want to do, but partner with them and make it simple. Do less with less and get out of the way.

How do you hold them accountable and set the appropriate measurements? First, go back to the items that link directly to their business strategy. Look at the top three HR priorities identified from Chapter 6 and establish performance measurements around these HR priorities that link directly to the business objectives. Next, determine what measurements make sense and set up a tracking mechanism. Determining a measurement that makes sense may be the biggest opportunity to have a great impact. Oftentimes the HR department gets accused of establishing arbitrary numbers that do not make sense for the business. To avoid doing this, you might need to start with a baseline test measurement so that you have real data behind what makes the most sense for the business. Examples follow about how two companies did each of these things. The first is an example of how an HR leadership team came up with arbitrary numbers and, later in the chapter, there is an example of an HR team taking time to establish a baseline so that the measurement made sense.

The first example is from a large, well-known manufacturing company. In this organization, HR objectives were set based on what was done in the prior year and an endless quest to do more and excel further and further. What this translated to was a lack of focus and unsuccessfully trying to accomplish numerous objectives, some that did not have a direct or obvious link to the business objectives.

Throughout the early 2000s, there was a perceived need to hire many entry-level professionals in anticipation of the mass exodus of the baby boomers (which never quite happened in the large droves that were anticipated). The senior HR leadership team established an objective which specified that of all external hires, 50% needed to be entry-level professionals. That objective made sense and worked well for a few years. The business leaders supported it and were able to make this mix of new hires work in their particular organizations.

As the years went on, there was a slow increase in the target number of this particular objective. The total number of entry-level professionals increased by a slight percentage each year. Eventually 70% of all external hires were expected to be entry-level professionals, even though this goal stopped making sense for the business. Not only had the economic climate impacted the rate at which baby boomers actually retired, but business conditions were also shifting. This drove the need for a greater number of experienced professionals than entry-level professionals. Because this company had hired such a high rate of entry-level professionals over the past several years, they now needed to balance that by increasing the number of experienced professionals that they hired.

Business leaders in the field began to question who came up with the objective that stated 70% of all external hires needed to be entry-level professionals. The directive had come from the senior vice president of HR. But the data about baby boomers retiring was no longer valid; it was old data that no longer supported the needs of the business. This put the field HR partners supporting the business leaders in an awkward position because they did not have an appropriate response to their leaders' question or a valid business case to support the objective. The senior vice president of HR had continued to increase the target for entry-level professionals because he wanted to have a workforce that appealed to younger generations and would sustain the organization for many years to come. That was an admirable and somewhat necessary thing to do. However, since having a workforce that appealed to younger generations was not the only pertinent factor impacting this business, that reasoning and that objective did not make complete sense. The business needed something different at this point, and it was incumbent upon the HR leadership team to have a realistic talent acquisition objective that supported what the business currently needed.

This was a measurement that did not mean anything to the leaders and was not one they were willing to support. They viewed it as an arbitrary objective that did not make sense and created unnecessary work for them. They were failing to hire people with the skills they needed, which drove the business in the wrong direction.

This example refers back to the importance of establishing focus and ensuring that the HR agenda, programs and objectives all directly link back to the business strategy. If they do not, then chances are strong that the business leaders will not support them. The measurements must mean something so that the leaders are committed to putting the programs into play and being held accountable for meeting the metrics.

From the example in Chapter 7 about the senior HR leadership team that imposed 60 objectives on the broader HR team, you can also see how some deadlines and metrics can become meaningless (which does not bode well for the HR team). To try and implement that many objectives and get business leaders to support them can become a futile effort. When you have an astronomical number of goals and objectives, it is very difficult to do anything well. People actually perform much better when they are focused instead of when they are trying to execute a myriad of objectives. What results is that nothing gets measured, or those things that do get measured are measured in a mediocre or inaccurate fashion. If business leaders see that HR cannot keep track of their own measurements, or that the integrity of the data that HR is measuring is questionable, they are not likely to be committed to the HR programs that they might truly need in their businesses, and HR loses credibility. The leaders will not hold themselves accountable if the HR team fails to hold themselves accountable.

That is why this concept is so vital. HR should work with leaders on creating measurements that mean something, and they should start with their own department. If you ensure that you have your own department in order and that your HR team can keep track of themselves and their responsibilities – that HR can hold themselves accountable - it will make it much easier for you to hold your clients accountable. Keeping track of yourselves as HR professionals and holding yourselves accountable to deadlines and measurements not only speaks volumes to your leaders but it also helps retain the trusted HR advisors that work in your company.

This next example is about a senior HR leader who did not hold herself accountable and was somewhat whimsical about deadlines. This ended up driving away two key trusted HR advisors from her team. This scenario starts in a Fortune 100 oil company at the beginning of a calendar year. Susie, the corporate vice president of workforce development, told her new director of talent development, Anna, that the enterprise-wide mentoring management system that her predecessor had procured and gotten approved needed to be implemented across the 100,000+ employee corporation by the end of the year. Anna gave this huge responsibility to her career development manager, Debbie, who was also new to the team.

They began by putting together a project plan to ensure that they had all the pieces in place that would enable the system to be operational by the end of the year. This was a very large project to manage as the system needed to be customized and updated with the current population information. It needed to be tested and piloted, and old systems that were being used needed to be shut down. This system was a large expense and effort for this company, and was being implemented because it supported the business need for knowledge transfer and would eventually enable the business to track the development of the population through active mentoring relationships. Anna and Debbie shared the implementation plan and schedule with their boss, Susie, as well as with the entire senior HR leadership team, and everyone agreed with the path forward.

As the year progressed, things remained on schedule. Anna and Debbie regularly provided status updates to Susie so she was fully aware of the progress that was occurring and the planned path forward. Pilot groups began testing the system in July and August, and by October the first division of the company that was scheduled to go "live" on the system was ready. This would be the first of a three-phase, go-live plan.

At this time, Anna and Debbie planned another meeting with Susie. It was two weeks prior to the time that the first division was to implement the new system. This meeting was to update Susie on the status of the first go-live phase. Instead, Susie pulled the brakes on the entire plan. Despite all the planning, climate-setting and training that had occurred over the past ten months, despite the cross-business team that was assembled and had engaged a variety of business leaders from across the company in the testing, piloting and training efforts, Susie said that she did not feel that the corporation was ready. She felt that she needed to share the full plan with her peers on the senior HR leadership team as well as receive their final approval of the mentoring strategy.

As you might imagine, there was silence and surprise in the meeting room from Anna and Debbie. They were shocked because they had kept Susie informed about everything throughout the year and would not have proceeded if they had known that the senior HR leadership team had not approved the mentoring strategy. Anna actually questioned Susie about the approval of the senior HR leadership team and referenced a meeting earlier in the year at which she had reviewed the implementation plan with them. Susie agreed that yes, they approved it back then, but now that the system was ready to go live they needed to go back for assurance that these HR leaders were aware of the strategy and path forward.

Needless to say, the entire team from across the company that had been involved in the project for the prior ten months was very discouraged and disappointed by the news. And the division that was scheduled to go live in phase one was angry that the implementation had been put on hold. In fact, because the next senior HR leadership meeting would not be held until January of the following year, the entire implementation plan was pushed back significantly.

You are probably wondering why Susie pulled the brakes on this project. Although the actual reason is unknown, the best answer is that Susie is a somewhat disorganized individual who does not know how to effectively manage a department, keep a schedule, or meet deadlines. As a result, her team had a lot of starts and stops on very large efforts. They sometimes moved very quickly on things that ended up slowing to a halt and never culminating. (This was an obvious feature of the prior example about the mentoring management system.)

Debbie, the career development manager, left the company one month later because she could not work under those conditions. She had worked arduously for almost an entire year on a project that, she was told, was high priority with a deadline that must be met. Since she was a person of high integrity and met deadlines consistently, especially those that had such a huge impact on the business, she could not come to terms with the fact that the project had been delayed indefinitely.

Despite all the hard work that had gone into meeting the original deadline, the delay was not a surprise to the company's business leaders who knew Susie's style. The people who knew her laughed it off because they typically did not take anything that she or her team did seriously. Unfortunately, this was a surprise for Anna and Debbie, who had joined her team at the beginning of that year and not familiar with their boss's pattern of behavior.

This example continues on because it took Anna a bit longer to realize the consequences of working with a leader who does not have respect for meeting deadlines. Anna spent the next eight months doing many other large projects and putting a lot of effort into creating many new programs, most of which did not go anywhere. She finally stopped taking action on directives from Susie and noticed that things just miraculously were forgotten. For example, Susie asked Anna to investigate creating a career portal from which employees could get information on career development. She wanted to have this portal be the "one-stop shopping" place where employees could access all things related to career development. She wanted the plethora of career development systems that were being used out in the businesses to be combined into one. Anna took lots of notes, left her boss's office and put the notes in a folder that she had labeled "Grand Ideas". Three months later, she advanced into a new assignment in the company and nothing ever came up again on the career portal idea, or on any of the many projects in her "Grand

Ideas" folder. In fact, Anna left the company within the next year and, sadly enough, the mentoring management system was still not fully deployed across the corporation.

This is a perfect example of what not to do. When the business leaders witnessed this type of behavior coming from HR, they thought of it as a joke. Why? Because they heard that the mentoring management system would be fully deployed by the end of the year and that they would need to start tracking their mentoring relationship metrics at that time, yet by the end the following year, when the system was still not fully deployed, the leaders no longer had faith in the original timeline or future timelines. Though this had been a meaningful project, something that supported their business objectives and they felt good about doing, the fact that the HR team responsible for it could not get their act together caused the leaders to lose all confidence in this group.

Sadly enough for this team, it became a company-wide joke. The deadlines were arbitrary and the leaders knew it. Unfortunately, this caused them to have little confidence in any of the metrics that this HR team requested or required, even if the metrics supported business objectives. They instead focused on other meaningful, non-HR measurements. Remember: What gets measured gets done, and the HR team should hold themselves accountable for their own measurements and data before requesting the same of their clients.

Despite the nonsensical nature of the prior examples and the sad state of this particular HR team, there is a perfect example of how HR can and does successfully create meaningful measurements for themselves and their clients. This example comes from a mid-sized software development company that, within a given year, had a very focused HR agenda and strategy to execute. One of this company's key objectives was to develop high-potential successors for critical positions. Some of their senior leaders were approaching retirement in the coming years and wanted to ensure that they had successors ready to fill these roles when they became vacant. Because the company had an executive development program in place, and there were many mid-level leaders who completed this program, the executive leaders believed that they had a solid pool of potential candidates from which to choose.

However, when they started to assess the employees who had completed the program, they realized that more than half were not of the caliber required to fill some of the executive level positions. The program was a big investment in the employees. Those who went through it received two weeks of focused classroom training, group mentoring, an executive coach, and also worked on a year-long strategic project. Yet they were not all of the appropriate caliber to be future executive leaders. There was never a target set for the total number of employees to participate in the program; leaders nominated their employees to participate without much forethought. However, now that the business needs were shifting and there was a focused need to develop successors, some targeted development of employees was required.

The HR leaders and business leaders decided that moving forward, this program would only be offered to a small number of select, high-potential employees. The HR leaders could have randomly picked a number that was smaller than the average number of employees who had participated in the past, but because they wanted the number to mean something to the business leaders, they decided to use the first year of this new focus to set a baseline metric.

As a starting point, HR advisors worked with their divisional vice presidents to select the top five employees within a certain range of leadership from each division to participate in the program for the upcoming year. This totaled 30 people. After these 30 people completed the program, they assessed how much they developed in certain areas, how well they performed during the development program, and how truly viable they were as potential successors for executive leaders. This evaluation was done using 360-degree leadership assessments and performance reviews. Each employee was discussed during an executive level talent review meeting and 20 employees were deemed potential successors. Although all 20 would not necessary make it to the top, that target number was decided upon because it provided two-to-three potential successors for each of the top positions.

Based on this information, the metric that was established for the following year was that 20 leaders would participate in the program moving forward. This was a meaningful metric. The following year another step was added to the process of deciding the most appropriate number of leaders to participate in the program - a review of all the potential senior leadership positions that could be opening up in the next two years. This was done to assess whether there was a need to include a few more leaders in the program based on a specific future need to fill a vacant position. Clearly this was a measurement that HR could easily hold business leaders accountable for because not only were the leaders involved in establishing the measurement (which created significant buy-in), but it made complete sense because it fully supported what the business needed.

Another good example of a meaningful measurement is a follow-up to a previous example about the manufacturing company that had the goal that 70% of all external hires needed to be entry-level hires. As the business leadership teams began to push back on this number, the HR leadership realized it needed to make an adjustment and come up with something that made more sense given the business needs. They first put a halt on all entry-level hiring for a three-month period, then went back to each business's senior vice president to find out what their specific hiring needs would be for the coming year. Each business's HR leader returned to the senior HR leadership team with the number of positions and skill mix needed for their business. Based on this data, the team decided that the minimum corporate-wide objective would be 25% of new hires in each business were to be entry-level professionals. Beyond that, the businesses could hire as best fit their needs. Though some businesses needed to reach a higher percentage, 25% was a ratio that all the businesses could support and a performance measurement for which their leaders could be held accountable. Although this seems like a simple solution (and it really is!), it is clear that many HR organizations do not take the time to set measurements that are meaningful to the business. They often end up without leadership support and unable to meet the targeted end state.

As we conclude with Principle V, you hopefully have a much clearer vision of what it means to get out of the way. It does not mean take a back seat and ignore what is going on around you but, instead, that you should do your very best to create simple processes and simple measurements that mean something. You should set the guidelines, provide strong counsel and solid advice, and then let your clients run their businesses using what you have provided as guidelines and boundaries. With simple processes, and measurements that hold them accountable to meaningful outcomes, you can step aside and watch them make the most of all the guidance you have provided to them as their trusted HR advisor.

APPLY THIS

"Do Less With Less" Tip Sheet

To ensure that you are focused on doing less with less, develop a monthly list of the HR "to do" items. This should mirror the HR Calendar of Events you created during Principle II. Each month review the list of items with yourself and your team and ask the following questions:

- Does the item on the list support a business objective?
- If yes, which business objective does it support?
- If not, cross it off your current to do list and put it on a "parking lot" list of items to consider for the following year.

By executing this simple process on a monthly basis, you can ensure that you are doing only what must be done to support the business and not falling into the trap of unnecessarily adding more to your list of things to do (and to your clients' lists).

This document is available for download at:
www.trustedadvisorreaderspage.com

HR Objective Tracking Template

Use this template to track the HR objectives and metrics for which leaders are held accountable. It can be used for your own internal HR tracking or as a method of sharing status with your clients (the author's recommendation is to go with the latter).

Sample HR Calendar of Events

HR Objective	Links to which of the top 3 HR priorities for the year	Links to which business objective	Target Metric	Owner	Status - Month
S A M P L E — O B J E C T I V E S					
Career discussions to be held with all high-potential employees	Retain 100% of high-potential talent	Develop robust pipeline of leaders for future business growth	Career discussions conducted with 100% of all high-potentials	Leaders	30% complete - March
Ensure adequate number of entry-level professionals in workforce skill mix	Acquire appropriate level of talent to support business needs	Ensure programs are fully staffed with appropriate skill mix to support program deliverables	At least 25% of all external hires should be entry-level professionals	Leaders	10% -March

This template is available for download at:
www.trustedadvisorreaderspage.com

AUTHOR'S NOTE:
PRINCIPLE V

I consulted with an HR director at a mid-sized company on one of the key concepts in Principle V: What Gets Measured Gets Done. This organization had HR objectives in place but because they had not established measurements that had any meaning to the leaders, they were not able to hold the leaders accountable for any of the measurements. Similar to many of the examples shared in the prior chapters, I worked with the HR director and his team on a collaborative effort to establish metrics with their organizational leaders. By working in partnership with the leaders, the measurements that were established had meaning for them and the HR team.

After establishing the appropriate performance measurements for the leaders, we created a consistent business rhythm in which to track the objectives and report back to the leaders about whether they were being met. This project was the first step for this team.

The next step further held leaders accountable by including their progress in their individual performance objectives. Therefore, if they did not meet their commitments, there would be a potential impact on their performance rating. This step took some time to implement because they needed to develop an accurate method by which performance ratings would be impacted. However, by ensuring that the measurements had meaning to the leaders, it was received with little resistance.

ENCOURAGE EXPECTATION

As human resources professionals, you rarely encourage anyone to expect anything in the workplace environment, right? This is especially true in U.S. companies where employment contracts are not common and nothing is guaranteed. Many of you probably cringe when you hear that employees "expect" a raise or a promotion or a certain performance rating. Expectations are probably not something you promote.

It is now time to shift your thinking. Not about expectations of what you or your employees will receive from your employer, but in regard to what you expect from your clients and what they expect from you.

Encourage them to expect the best from you, their trusted HR advisor, and the HR team, at all times. That not only holds you accountable but also projects their positive expectations onto you and vice versa. They will get what they expect and you will get the same. Now is the time to encourage everyone to expect only the best.

CHAPTER 11

EXPECTING THE BEST

CAN YOU FEEL THE SHIFT OCCURING? HOPEFULLY, now that you have learned about and worked on the first five Bridge Principles and are applying them consistently in your daily work practices, you and your clients should be able to feel the shift. It is a movement from behaviors, attitudes and practices that created barriers, to those of trusted advisors. It is a shift that should now be visible to you and your clients. The gap that separated you and your HR team from the support that your clients need to be successful and achieve business results is now closing. The gap is closing because you have made the effort to shift your own behaviors. The shift will become permanent as you continue to practice the Bridge Principles and foster an environment that encourages positive, expectant attitudes.

An expectant attitude is one of having feelings of anticipation about a person or occurrence. People tend to live up to their expectations, and their environment becomes a mirror of their beliefs, attitudes and expectations. Positive attitudes and expectations yield positive results; negative attitudes and expectations yield negative results. The world tends to give back what you expect, which is why you need to expect the very best.

If you go back to Principle I, in which you had to check your attitude, that was the premise for encouraging expectation and continuing to close the gap. You are now using behaviors and principles that support being a trusted advisor, and you can now anticipate positive outcomes when you are interacting with your clients. Even in the most difficult situations, you have proven and continue to prove that you are a trusted advisor and can work with and through any circumstance with them. You are thinking "How?" instead of instantly saying "No," and looking for the creative pathways to "Yes," while at the same time you have enough courage to say "No" when that is what your clients need to hear. These behaviors and actions allow you to expect the best of yourself and encourage your clients to expect continued trusted advisor performance and conduct from you.

This next example is about Mike, a trusted HR advisor at a Fortune 100 information technology company who appeared in a previous example. The previous example was of Mike at an earlier stage in his career. This is another example of Mike, at a later career stage, demonstrating his trusted advisor skills. He spent 16 years with large companies before starting his own company. Although he consistently behaved as a trusted advisor throughout his career, it was during his last six months in the corporate world that he clearly utilized the Bridge Model. He did this to effectively influence and support his client group in bridging the gap to their success.

Mike's final assignment came at a time when he knew he was going to be leaving the company soon, but still wanted to have a positive impact on the leaders he was supporting. He took over as the HR director supporting the chief technology officer (CTO) and an organization of 15,000 engineers and scientists. He was replacing an individual who had not been a trusted HR advisor and who had isolated many of the leaders within the CTO's organization. Mike knew that reengaging the leaders on this team would be a challenging task.

As we saw in an earlier example, Mike had been using Bridge Principles throughout his career. Although he did not call them that, the practices were the same. He was a very well-respected, high-potential and highly-thought-of HR advisor. He was sought out for various HR roles, and leaders who had worked with him in the past repeatedly wanted to work with him again. He had been the HR representative supporting the CTO many years earlier, when they were both at lower levels in the company, and she wanted him to support her again in this much larger role. The CTO is the person to whom, in the earlier example, Mike had given some difficult feedback. Because Mike had distinguished himself to her and many other leaders as a true trusted advisor consistently throughout his career, and had maintained the relationship, she sought him out to work with her again. The way Mike conducted himself with the CTO and her team was exactly the way he conducted himself for most of his career. That is why he was regularly requested to fill vacant HR roles.

Mike's entrance into this role was welcomed by the leaders of this organization, and the CTO's group was excited to have him join the team. Many of them had worked with him previously and were eager to have him as their primary HR support due to their poor experience with the previous HR director. They expected the best from Mike and he always delivered.

Despite the fact that Mike already knew half the CTO staff members, he set up his first 90-day plan using the Build Your Base concepts of checking his attitude and beginning with the end in mind. Mike knew he already had the appropriate attitude to be a trusted HR advisor. Yet, there were people on the new team who did not know him well so he needed to demonstrate his trusted advisor practices to build solid relationships with everyone. Despite the fact that he was planning to leave the company within the next year, he went through the exercise of ensuring that he had the appropriate positive attitude for his new assignment. He wanted an open, trusting, productive partnership with this team. He experienced that type of relationship with most departments and leaders he had supported in the past and knew what those relationships felt and looked like. He focused on that image as he began his 90-day plan. The first 30-60 days were allocated to what he called his "introductory road show". Mike scheduled one-on-one meetings with each person who reported directly to the CTO and made visits to all the major sites where the engineers and scientists were located. He spent this time getting to know each of the leaders, their departmental issues and challenges and their business priorities.

Mike approached these meetings with an open mind. His only objective (which he stated during each meeting) was to listen and understand the issues the business leaders and their teams faced. Throughout these meetings and one-on-one discussions with many of the employees, Mike not only practiced the principle of building his base but also responding responsibly. In fact, there was one meeting in particular in which he became the target of some difficult feedback. Mike's predecessor had spearheaded some decisions and implemented some procedures regarding hiring practices that were causing the leaders at one location a lot of hardship. The process for hiring employees at a certain level had become cumbersome due to excessive reviews through the HR chain and an extra-long interviewing cycle. The leaders felt that they had lost many good candidates due to this process. At one point, Mike started to feel defensive and as if he needed to have all the answers and to defend his HR colleague and the HR function as a whole. This resulted in the beginnings of some reacting on his part, yet because of his self-awareness, he recognized the defensive feeling and decided to resort to his version of the "two hour rule"; that is, he used what he called the "defuse rule".

Earlier in his career, Mike might have continued reacting to the leaders in a defensive or argumentative fashion. He felt like he was being attacked and he used to believe that when attacked, one must defend. However, over the years, he had learned to employ his "defuse rule", and so he turned his attention to defusing the situation. He was not rude or unresponsive but instead went fully into listen mode, trying to view the situation from the perspective of those who were upset. His responses were, "Let me see what we can do to address this," and "Why don't we talk about this further one-on-one and see what we can do to address this situation in a more efficient and effective way?" His objective was to neutralize the situation in the public forum, take some time (at least two hours) for those involved to gather their thoughts, and also, if necessary, to cool down. By employing this practice in the current situation, Mike was able to work with the frustrated leaders (in a separate meeting) on a new, more effective process that was later disseminated to the larger team.

Mike's self-awareness and ability to keep calm and not react also enabled him to practice the principle of Influence Impeccably in a flawless manner. Because of his ability to keep his defenses in check, listen, view the situation from his clients' perspective, and suggest working a solution outside the larger meeting, he was able to take control of the situation. By doing this and then following up and working on a resolution with the leaders, he was able to effectively and impeccably influence their path forward. Had he remained defensive and reacted, he likely would not have gained the necessary respect required to exert influence with the group outside of that meeting setting.

After Mike finished his "introductory road show", he spoke with the CTO and her direct reports about the key issues that were presented to him, what he understood to be the key business objectives, and a proposal for how HR could support the engineering organization in meeting their mission.

Mike's actions during the first 90 days set the tone for many more good things to come. He demonstrated that he was there to serve the business; not that he was a servant but that he was there to serve and support them in their business objectives. Gaining this respect enabled Mike to continue distinguishing himself as a trusted HR advisor.

What he continued to do throughout his time in this role demonstrates the fluidity of the Bridge Model. He did not simply build his base for the first 90 days and then assume the relationships were strong enough for him to sit back and do nothing else. He nurtured the relationships by continuing to partner with the business leaders and getting involved in a proactive manner. Mike did not sit back and wait for the phone to ring and problems to be presented to him; he was always out and about, engaged with his clients and the business leaders. He held regular team and one-on-one meetings with employees and visited the sites he supported on a consistent basis. He was considered a familiar face and someone the employees felt comfortable talking to and were accustomed to seeing.

HR personnel often get a reputation for showing up only when things are wrong or when people are being disciplined or punished, so employees tend to run and hide when they see their HR partners or know they are in the vicinity. Mike made a consistent effort to reach out to employees, get to know them and have casual conversations with them so that they looked forward to seeing him. Because he did this, his presence was considered "normal". They expected to see him for good reasons and, because he typically showed up for good reasons, he encouraged this type of expectation from the workforce. This is stark contrast to a comment given by a senior leader at a government agency who was asked what he thought of human resources professionals. His response was, "I avoid them at all costs." This individual was obviously not dealing with a trusted advisor like Mike.

Because Mike built up such a solid reputation for himself and established enduring relationships with all levels of employees and leaders, he had a much easier time exerting influence at all levels in the organization. He also had a much easier time saying "No" to his leaders and guiding them toward a different, more productive pathway. A good example of this was Mike's involvement with the reorganization of the engineering department in response to a large-scale organizational restructuring that was occurring outside of their department due to a shift in customer needs and business priorities. Because the engineers were assigned to various programs out in the different divisions of this company, the entire engineering department needed to adapt their structure to the overall organizational structure. By doing this, they were able to operate in a manner that facilitated an effective supply of talent and skills to the various divisions of the company.

Although there was no threat of anyone losing their job through this reorganization, Mike was seasoned enough to know that most employees would get concerned when they heard about a reorganization – if not about losing their jobs then about where they would end up as a result of the restructuring. He knew that the best way to deal with this was to be transparent and open and let the employees know what was going on. He knew to not be secretive but instead to share information and help the employees see the change as an opportunity to grow, develop, and advance their careers. Although not everyone on the CTO's staff was receptive to this idea, they trusted Mike enough to get on board with it. As he and the senior leadership team worked out a schedule to design and implement a new organizational structure, they included regular progress updates to all employees. They also planned for regular meetings that all leaders would be required to conduct with their direct reports regarding the status of the reorganization. This design ensured the flow of effective and consistent communication. Mike made himself and his team readily available to support leaders in these meetings and to answer employee questions and concerns. In fact, he put one of his senior HR managers in charge of doing nothing but responding to employee and leader questions and concerns about the reorganization.

It should be noted that one of the other things that made Mike truly stand out as a trusted advisor was that he "walked the talk" and required the same of the other HR professionals on his team. He set very clear expectations up front about what was and was not acceptable behavior. Many of his dos and don'ts are reflected in Chapters 7 and 8. As part of his first 90 days in the role, he moved some of his staff around so that only those who exhibited true trusted advisor behaviors were dealing directly with the clients. Other individuals were put in positions better suited to their strengths or exited from the company. He did not waste time, as he knew that if he wanted to have a strong, positive impact on this group, he needed a team of the strongest players.

Not all of you have the luxury of moving people around and surrounding yourself with the best of the best available talent, however, at a minimum, it is important that you make your expectations known and deliver consequences for behaviors that do not meet those expectations. That will demonstrate to your clients and the other people on your team that you are quite serious not only about being a trusted advisor yourself, but also about having a team of true trusted advisors to support your clients.

You can probably imagine that Mike's strategies for the restructure of the engineering department resulted in a successful outcome for this organization. Although not everyone was happy with the end result, a majority of the workforce was comfortable, and more importantly, throughout the four months of change and flux, restructuring and reprocessing, the employees were all very productive. Mike's behaviors had a direct impact on their productivity. He continued to keep relationships strong and remained a visible face of honesty for all levels of employees. He responded openly and required the same of all players involved in the restructuring. He continued to influence leaders about the best paths to take, and then got out of the way and let the leaders be leaders and run their businesses. This made all the difference in the reputation of the human resources department. Those in the engineering department actually credited HR with the smoothness of the restructuring. How often is that the case? Not often enough, and it's certainly something all HR professionals should strive to achieve more consistently. Business leaders typically blame the HR department for creating cumbersome processes that prevent actions from flowing and for being the reason a restructuring does not go smoothly. Mike's team did a brilliant job of countering the "typical" and creating a new expectation of how HR professionals should behave and demonstrating the results those behaviors produce.

It should also be noted here that Mike and his team were not a group of "yes people"; they did not let the organizational leaders do whatever they pleased. In fact, they probably said "Yes" very few times throughout this process, focusing instead on "How?" and working on creative pathways to get to the "Yes" that worked best for the business and the employees. The result was that HR was credited with a successful transition. Bravo to Mike and his stellar team.

Mike left the company a few months after he got through the

reorganization. He knew it was time to move on and do something different, and that was a huge loss to the company. They tried to keep him but his desire to leave was not about the company but about spreading his message and good efforts in a broader manner. Throughout his many years at that company, Mike left a big footprint across the company. Even when he knew he was going to be leaving, he consistently demonstrated the behaviors and attitudes of a trusted HR advisor. He also had a significant positive impact on many of the HR professionals who worked for him. Hopefully they are following in his footsteps and continuing to walk the same walk he did as a true trusted advisor.

Mike's example shows that if you practice all the Bridge Principles on a consistent basis and keep them in the forefront of your mind as you interact with your clients, you can close that gap between gatekeeper and trusted advisor. Consistently acting in the ways that Mike did will encourage that positive expectation from your clients as it did from his clients. They expected the best from him, and he expected the best from himself and his team, and that is typically what everyone got – the best.

As you can also tell from Mike's example, reputation is a vitally important piece of the puzzle. He was sought-after because the business leaders had positive experiences with him in the past, and they continued to hear of others who had positive experiences with him. But no matter what you have done in the past, if you make the decision to start fresh and are committed to being a trusted advisor, you can do it. You can begin with the end in mind and follow the Bridge Principles to build a solid reputation so that you can be the one who is sought after and singled out.

Closing the gap between gatekeeper and trusted advisor is also about understanding what leaders truly think of HR as a whole. You are the face of HR, and even if they think very differently about you, personally, than what they think about the HR function as a whole, it still impacts you.

After speaking with many trusted HR and business leaders, the general consensus about what organizational leaders think of HR can be summed up with this analogy (given graciously by one of the interviewees for this book): "I love my congressman but I hate Congress." Most leaders loved their particular HR partner but were much less fond of the HR department as a whole. Why is this? The general consensus is that HR, as a whole, has not done a good job of collectively changing the age-old perception that they are compliance cops instead of true partners and trusted advisors. Individual HR partners make concerted efforts to act as trusted advisors but often get blocked by their own processes or rules (hence the sentiment of loving a particular HR partner but not the entire HR function).

Perceptions of HR professionals also change depending upon the level of the leader. Senior leaders tend to have a greater appreciation and understanding of HR professionals and the strategic value they provided than lower-level leaders. They typically deal with the most senior leaders of HR who focus on strategic issues, and this may shelter them from everyday HR issues that occur at lower levels. Lower-level leaders have less appreciation and less tolerance for HR, and this is probably where HR professionals can have the most influence and need to do the most work to change the perception.

Another theme is that the perception of HR depends on the reputation of the most senior HR person in the business. If there is respect for that person, then there is respect for the HR organization as a whole. However, that respect can quickly be lost if the larger HR team is lacking and the senior HR leader does not take action to get a solid team in place.

Regularly practicing the Bridge Principles as you are interacting with your clients will help create a more positive perception of HR efforts. One step at a time, one HR professional at a time, Build Your Base, Respond Responsibly, Influence Impeccably, Distinguish Yourself, Get Out Of The Way and Encourage Expectation. You have the keys and it is in your power to have a positive influence on the perceptions of human resources and HR teams far and wide.

CHAPTER 12

SO THEREFORE WHAT?

JOHN, THE VICE PRESIDENT AND GENERAL MANAGER of a $2.5B business, was considered a difficult leader to support. He expected the highest quality performance and results from his team and all those who worked with him. As the leader of such a large business, he had a lot of demands of his time and attended countless meetings at which he was presented with endless information about a great assortment of topics. Typically the presenters would be looking for him to make a decision on a project, use of funds, or the advancement of some program. John's question was always the same: "So therefore what?" He wanted to know what all this information meant to his business, and if the presenter could not answer that question, it would likely be the end of the meeting.

This chapter is about the trusted HR advisor's ability to answer that question. As another means to encouraging expectation, trusted advisors need to be able explain how HR programs and initiatives support the business objectives and why they should be implemented. You must be able to answer that question and it is probably best to answer it at the beginning of a meeting.

Jean was the HR leader who supported John's organization, and she made the mistake of not having that answer available when proposing the implementation of a new rewards and recognition program for employees. She could not articulate how or why this would be beneficial for the business, only that it was something that was being required by the corporate headquarters HR team. John said that he would not support the effort and would not allow it to be carried out in his business until he had a solid, understandable business justification for doing so.

This only happened once. Jean quickly learned that to say, "It is a corporate requirement" was not enough (nor should it ever be enough) and quickly learned the importance of being able to answer John's question of, "So therefore what?" In fact, she started to present that information to John first. At the next meeting, she titled the presentation "Rewards and Recognition Program", and the second chart was titled, "So Therefore What?" and presented the answer to that question. It detailed the business outcome of implementing the program and also the outcome of not implementing the program.

This was a fantastic exercise that Jean then required of all her team members so that they would develop the habit of providing business justification for all HR initiatives. If there was not a business justification behind the HR program, it would not go forward for approval. This sometimes caused difficulty when a program had been initiated by the corporate headquarters HR team without appropriate business justification. Jean requested this information from the corporate headquarters HR team and instead of seeing her request for business justification as a positive, the corporate team interpreted it as the inability of the field HR team to influence their leadership. In reality, backing up initiatives with a business justification is an important part of being able to influence.

To many of you, this probably seems so basic that there is no point in emphasizing it. However, the fact is that there are many HR professionals who do not establish solid business reasoning for their initiatives. They develop and implement programs because they think they will benefit the workforce and that is the extent of their justification. However, unless you can show your business leaders, in detailed factual terms, how something will benefit their business and their workforce, it is a moot point.

That is the basic significance of the "So therefore what?" question. There is also a larger meaning in the context of the six Bridge Principles. Now that you know and understand all of the principles and concepts related to being a trusted advisor, ask yourself this question: So therefore what? What does this all mean?

What it really boils down to is whether you know and can define the role of the trusted HR advisor and whether you know what is expected of someone in that role. This book has given you a variety of examples about how trusted advisors behave and perform - examples of what to do and what not to do. Ultimately it comes down to finding a balance that works for you and the particular clients you support. Each client is different and has different needs. Your ability to assess and respond to the needs of your particular client group in their particular business is vital to your success and how you are perceived. The beauty of the Bridge Principles is that they are universal and fluid. It does not matter if you are supporting a large business in growth mode or a small business in steady-state mode, the use of the Bridge Principles as your foundation will help you become a trusted advisor and succeed in your HR role.

So, therefore, what are the most critical themes realized through the development of the Bridge Model and the surplus of wisdom imparted by the trusted HR advisors and business leaders interviewed for this book? First, remember that it is not about you; it is about your clients and supporting their business objectives, strategies and growth. Without the business, the HR function would not exist.

A great example of this comes from Harrison, an HR director who supported the chief financial officer (CFO) of a large aerospace company. Harrison was a very high-energy, fast-moving individual, and although the CFO was energized as well, he did not express it outwardly as Harrison did. The CFO's demeanor was very calm and laid back.

Early on in this relationship, Harrison and his CFO would have one-on-one meetings in which Harrison would run through a list of items that he needed to address and review with the CFO. This often left his client looking like a deer in the headlights. They were on different wavelengths when it came to the best way use the time in those meetings. Because Harrison was extremely perceptive, and noticed that he was the one doing all the talking and directing the flow of their meetings, he decided to shift his approach. He knew that these meetings were not supposed to be about him and what he needed to accomplish from an HR perspective, but were supposed to be about the CFO and what he needed from HR to support his business. Harrison decided to start every meeting by asking the CFO what was on his mind and what he wanted to discuss during their time together. Now the meetings focused on what was pertinent to the CFO at that particular time. Sometimes he would not have anything to discuss and would defer to Harrison, who then went through his own list of items.

The point here is, again, to remember that it is not about HR but about the clients. Observe the energy level of the people you are supporting and interacting with and do your best to mirror it and pace yourself. If you do this, you will avoid creating anxiety for them, isolating them, or overwhelming them with things that might not be on their radar screen or of key importance to them.

Another "So therefore what?" is to speak the same language as your clients. This was touched upon through the information presented in Principle III, Influence Impeccably, about repeating what your clients say in their terminology. Hopefully, you are now aware that you cannot have credibility or influence if you are not speaking in their language. You should avoid "HR speak" as much as possible and, instead, speak the business language.

Along those same lines as speaking your clients' language is the need to understand your company's financial statements. This really is not an option if you truly want to speak your clients' language. One of the HR vice presidents interviewed for this book spent countless days with the CFO of her organization in order to fully understand and appreciate the financial position of the business. She did this early on in her assignment as the HR vice president so that she could jump into her role with a solid comprehension of her company's finances.

If you do not understand your financial statements and how your company makes money, then you cannot speak the language of your company leaders or provide adequate HR support. Unfortunately, many HR professionals regard understanding financial statements as an option rather than a requirement of their profession. After all, there are finance professionals to handle that part of the business. Although that is true, remember that you should be focused on what is important to your clients, and the financial standing of the business is often their most important concern. Therefore, it should also be one of your most important concerns.

By implementing and practicing the six principles, you should now be in the position of a performance consultant more so than in the position of a compliance cop. A performance consultant works with their leaders on implementing sustainable solutions to meet business needs. Being risk-averse and compliance-focused does not make you a trusted and respected HR partner; being a performance consultant does.

Jeremy, an HR leader in a financial services company, shared a great example of how even simple acts can be indicative of the performance consultant role. The vice president of sales in Jeremy's company received some negative feedback and complaints about inappropriate conduct on the part of some members of the sales force in the field. He went to Jeremy and requested a four-hour refresher training for the sales force on customer intimacy. This was the quick and easy solution, but because these were seasoned sales professionals, it seemed unlikely that refresher training was going to have a great impact, get to the root of the issue, or provide lasting results. Acting as a performance consultant, Jeremy worked with the vice president to come up with a more sustainable solution which required a more solid understanding of the complaints and the situations surrounding them.

At first, as you might suspect, the vice president resisted Jeremy's idea because he truly was seeking a quick fix. Being a trusted HR advisor, Jeremy did not back down, and explained that even if they did the refresher training, chances were fairly certain that this would not solve the problem and that they would need to address the situation more comprehensively to implement a sustainable change. Jeremy was not trying to make the situation more complex, but wanted to be sure the appropriate issue was addressed instead of forcing the entire sales force to participate in training they had already completed.

It would have been easier for Jeremy to agree to conduct the training, but being a trusted advisor means acting as a performance consultant, even if extra effort and extra resources are required. Doing this consistently establishes you as a performance consultant for your clients and encourages them to expect you to act as such.

The final "So therefore what?" really summarizes the topic: Let your leaders be leaders. This has been mentioned numerous times throughout the book and it is so vitally important that it is worth mentioning again. Your job is not to run their business and lead for them. Your job is to be their trusted advisor, to partner with them, to establish guidelines for them, to build credibility so that they heed your advice, and to have faith that they know how to run their business. It is not your job to tell them what to do or how to run their business. Yes, they will make mistakes, and if you believe they are on the path to a mistake, then it is your job to alert them about that. But ultimately they get to decide if they want to make the mistake.

Somewhere along the line, some HR professionals decided it was their job to tell their leaders what they could and could not do instead of providing guidance and letting them make the decisions. Instead, let them lead. Be there alongside them and be their partner, but by all means, let them do what they were hired and trained to do, even if it means they need to learn some hard lessons.

As an HR professional, you are probably thinking that you may need to cover yourself in those types of situations. You may be thinking, "What if they do something that is unethical or potentially illegal? Even if I advised them otherwise, what if they do it anyway and then I get in trouble?" You all know the solution to this situation: documentation. Document your conversation with your client or send your client an email specifying the advice you gave. Hopefully those situations are the exceptions and not the rule, and you are not running around every day trying to cover yourself. Believe in yourself, as the trusted advisor, and believe in your client, as a trusted leader. Remember to encourage expectation of only the best and it is guaranteed that the best is what you will receive.

As we recap the Bridge Model, it might be helpful to look at it from another viewpoint. Jim is an HR vice president of a manu-facturing company. He provided a great synopsis of the behaviors he feels are required of HR professionals if they are to stop being viewed as gatekeepers. Without even being aware of the Bridge Model, he went into great detail about what he felt were key con-cepts for trusted advisors. As he talked about them, it became clear that they aligned exactly to the Bridge Model.

The first item he talked about was being attuned to and under-standing the business. One should understand the financial state-ments and how the business operates. This starts building credibility. Next, one should understand and meet clients' needs. These needs vary depending on the client, so it is vital that you understand the client-specific needs and can meet them; that is the foundation of building credibility. Both of these items are key aspects of the Build Your Base concepts that include getting to know your client's vision, strategy, and what they need to be successful.

The next item Jim talked about was building up trust and rap-port. This includes things like responding responsibly and establish-ing a history of meeting clients' needs. Building this trust and rap-port also includes effective influencing and knowing when and how to exert appropriate influence on your clients. HR professionals who have long-standing service in their company have that type of his-tory behind them, so their credibility precedes them. The example of Mike in Chapter 11 demonstrates this clearly. He had the history of meeting clients' needs and he carried it with him to each new assign-ment. However, even if you do not have the benefit of such a history, and are brand new to an organization, you can quickly build up this type of trust and rapport.

The following scenario illustrates how this can be done excep-tionally well. Kelley, a junior HR partner, was hired as a new employee to provide HR support to a 600-person organization. The former HR partner had been removed because the leaders could not work with her. Suffice it to say that this individual practiced almost every one of the "don't" behaviors outlined in Chapter 8.

Kelley came in with ten years of experience and a very strong, confident personality. She had the authentic behaviors and attitudes required to be a trusted advisor and the first thing she focused on was understanding and trying to meet her clients' needs. They had an immediate and strong need for a responsive HR partner who would help them simplify some complex and cumbersome processes that had been in place for a long time.

In her first three weeks on the job, Kelley quickly worked to assess the situation and respond to these needs. She could not alter all of the procedures that they wanted to change, but she was able to make headway on a few of them. She also put a plan in place to partner with them on a longer-term fix for a few others, and because of this they were willing to accept her saying "No" to those that could not be changed.

By meeting these immediate needs quickly, Kelley got off to a strong start and on the right path with her clients. Kelley's credibility grew because she continued to partner with her clients and focus on what was best for their business. Doing this enabled her to swiftly become their trusted HR advisor. This example shows that it does not necessarily take long service to demonstrate trusted advisor status. What it takes is the right attitudes, behaviors and practices.

The last key item that Jim discussed was that HR professionals should have the courage to say and do the right thing which aligns with Principle III, Influence Impeccably and Principle IV, Distinguish Yourself. The ability to do this comes much more fluidly once the other items are in place and the credibility has been established. Although the Bridge Model is not linear, it is definitely more effective to build your base prior to trying to exert influence. Sometimes you do not have the luxury of that kind of time and have to come in and immediately start influencing your clients. Nonetheless, your effectiveness will be assessed based on your approach, your follow up, and whether, after the dust has settled, you take the time to work on (and continue to work on) the other Bridge Principles.

As is evident from the examples shared by Jim on moving from gatekeeper to trusted advisor, many of you have been practicing these key concepts throughout your career, though you may have been referring to them differently. They are not new concepts but they are easy to forget when you're busy. That is really the most important thing to take away from this book – to be aware and to remember. Care enough about how you and the entire HR profession are perceived to be aware of how you are behaving and to remember the Bridge Principles. Doing this will allow you and your clients to continually expect and receive only the best. And that really sums up the response to: "So therefore what?"

PRINCIPLE VI

APPLY THIS

"So Therefore What" Template

Use the attached sample charts as you are presenting a new HR initiative or program to your clients and trying to gain their support and buy-in.

PROGRAM NAME

- *BRIEF DESCRIPTION OF THE HR PROGRAM OR INITIATIVE YOU ARE PRESENTING.*

Slide 1

SO THEREFORE, WHAT?

- *STATE WHAT IMPACT THIS PROGRAM OR INITIATIVE WILL HAVE ON THE BUSINESS.*
- *USE NUMBERS, IF AVAILABLE/POSSIBLE (FOR EXAMPLE, THIS PROGRAM IS PROVEN TO INCREASE EMPLOYEE RETENTION RATES BY 5%).*

Slide 2

DETAILS OF PROGRAM

- *INCLUDE ALL RELEVANT INFORMATION ON THE PROGRAM AS WELL AS THE PLANNED IMPLEMENTATION SCHEDULE AND WHO IS RESPONSIBLE FOR VARIOUS TASKS.*

Slide 3

BUSINESS OBJECTIVE ALIGNMENT

- *INCLUDE INFORMATION ON THE BUSINESS OBJECTIVE OR OBJECTIVES THAT THIS PROGRAM ALIGNS TO AND SUPPORTS.*

Slide 4

These charts are available for download at:
www.trustedadvisorreaderspage.com

AUTHOR'S NOTE:
PRINCIPLE VI

An HR leader in a small research firm requested my services to support her team in regard to the principle of encouraging expectation. She felt that she and her HR team had a fairly solid reputation at her company, yet it still seemed as though minor, short-term HR mishaps were always the focus of the leaders. After a bit of investigating, we discovered that most of the HR mishaps were due to miscommunication within the small HR team. This was a team that mostly worked virtually, so they had minimal face-to-face time with each other. They did not always have insight into what other team members were working on and often made duplicate requests and communicated repeatedly about the same items to their clients (unbeknownst to the individual HR team members).

The first thing that needed to be done was to gain a clear understanding of what each HR team member was responsible for and then develop an internal reporting mechanism within the team to ensure that everyone was meeting these expectations. We instituted what they named the HRPR (Human Resources Program Review), which was a monthly videoconference meeting for all HR team members. During this meeting, they reported on the status of their own programs as well as the communication plan to status the workforce on these programs. This helped with some of the miscommunication to the leaders and the workforce.

The next step is where the principle of Encourage Expectation came into play. The HR leader of this team began using the "So therefore what" chart template to report to the senior leadership team about all the HR programs. She met with the senior business leaders on a quarterly basis to provide them with the status of the HR programs and objectives. By using the "So therefore what" template, she was able to share the most current impact of each HR program on the business objectives.

This clearly demonstrated to the senior leaders how the HR team was performing against expectations. The more the senior HR leader was able to answer the "So therefore what?" question, the more the business leadership team began expecting those types of results and performance from the HR team.

By implementing a monthly HR program review and consistent use of the "So therefore what" template, this HR team was able to begin encouraging the best expectations from themselves, and their business leaders began expecting the best from the HR team.

ENDING PROLOGUE

YOUR SEAT
HAS BEEN SAVED

You have reached the final chapter and are now at the beginning of a new path for yourself as an HR Professional. That is why this chapter is not called the Epilogue, but the Ending Prologue. Being committed to practicing the Bridge Principles and the related concepts enables HR professionals to alter the perceptions of being gatekeepers, barriers and roadblocks. That is the purpose of the Bridge Model and this book, to help change the perceptions, one HR person at a time. Somehow the perception was created that the HR department does not add value, creates more work, and makes easy things more difficult. This perception was created one HR person at a time. Therefore, the only way to swing the pendulum the other way is one person at a time.

The chapter is titled "Your Seat Has Been Saved" because the original title for this book was, *Are They Saving You a Seat at the Table? What Every HR Professional Must Do To Succeed Today.* The title changed for a variety of reasons, but I chose to head the final chapter with a version of this title because the entire premise of the

Bridge Model and bridging the gap between gatekeeper and trusted advisor will save you your seat at the table with your business leaders. If you are the trusted advisor, not only will you have a seat, but they will also be saving it for you.

This is your opportunity to be the bridge to your clients' success. Remember that the Bridge Model is not linear; it is fluid and requires movement consistently back and forth between each of the principles. If you must pick something to do first, then always go to Principle I, Build Your Base, and do it repeatedly, as required. The other principles are practiced repeatedly as well. Even if you work with the same group of clients for ten years, you continually have to be sure the foundation is solid; you should assess for cracks and splits and then work to fill them in and keep the foundation strong.

Trusted HR Advisors do this in the form of seeking feedback from their clients. They not only seek it but they listen to it and use it to their advantage. If you are not yet on a schedule of regularly seeking input from your clients, then start doing this. Go back to Chapter 7 and review the "start/stop/continue" model. Request this information from your clients on a regular basis - at least twice a year and more preferably, once a quarter. Keep track of what they are telling you and how you improve from one feedback discussion to the next.

Seeking regular feedback also helps you assess how you are doing in regard to the other Bridge Principles. Perhaps you not only ask for "start/stop/continue" feedback but for specific feedback on how you are responding to their needs, how effectively they see you exerting your influence, if they see you as "in the way" with complex processes, or if they see you as simplifying, doing less with less and partnering with them on creative pathways to "Yes". I recommend that you alternate your feedback processes so that perhaps in one quarter you get information on what you should start, stop and continue, and in another quarter you get information on how you are doing specifically in regard to each of the Bridge Principles. You can also seek feedback on the particular Bridge Principles that you want to improve upon. The choice is yours but the objective remains the same: seek feedback.

There are two final stories to share as this book concludes. This example sums up and is the culmination of how beneficial it will be to the HR profession if all HR professionals can be seen as trusted advisors to their clients. You may recall a few prior examples about Mike, and these that follow are also about Mike. As you know, he was a trusted, respected and sought-after HR advisor at the company where he worked. During an executive high-potential talent discussion in his company, Mike's name came up for discussion and, seated around the table were the top ten leaders of the company. Everyone knew Mike and everyone had something positive to say about him. When the meeting facilitator asked the question, "So, what is next for Mike? What are we going to do to continue to grow him?" someone said, "I'll take him," and then someone else raised their hand and said, "No, I'll take him," and someone else said, "No, I want him," and on it went, like a domino effect. *Every* person seated around that table said, "I'll take him!" He was the one they wanted and consistently was the one they asked for. Are you the one your business leaders are asking for? Hopefully that answer is "Yes."

Mike also was the role model for this chapter's title, "Your Seat Has Been Saved". This next example highlights the reason why. There was a strategic leadership meeting occurring in the business area that Mike supported. The meeting was scheduled for two full days and on both of those days, Mike had a previously scheduled personal commitment in the morning that could not be rescheduled. Therefore, he had to arrive approximately 15 minutes late on each day. When he arrived on the first day, at first glance it appeared that all the seats around the conference room table were taken. So he started to walk towards the outskirts of the room to sit in a chair next to some others who were seated there. It was then that the chief technology officer (the leader of the group he supported) called out to him and said, "Mike, up here, I saved you a seat." And, low and behold, there was an empty space at the table that Mike had not seen at first glance. This seat was next to the CTO. On day two when Mike walked in (again, 15 minutes late), there actually was a piece of paper on the table in front of an empty chair which said, "Saved For Mike." There were people seated at the perimeter of the conference table and lined up against the walls, and the message was clear: the empty seat at the table was saved for Mike. He was their trusted HR advisor and their partner and they wanted him at that table with them. He demonstrated and consistently practiced all of the principles and concepts discussed throughout this book. This paid off substantially for him and, in turn, for the business and the clients he supported. So, my HR friends, I ask you: Are they saving YOU a seat at the table? Hopefully that answer is now "Yes!"

REFERENCES

Ulrich. D., Brockbank, W., et al. (2008), HR Competencies: Mastery At The Intersection Of People And Business, Society for Human Resource Management: Alexandria, VA.

Watkins, M. (2003), The First 90 Days: Critical Success Strategies For New Leaders At All Levels, Harvard Business School Press: Boston, MA.

Welch, J. (2005), Winning, Harper Collins: New York, NY.

ABOUT THE AUTHOR

Andria Corso is an esteemed organizational and leadership development coach and Strategic Human Resources consultant with areas of expertise in career and leadership development, talent and succession management, and executive coaching. She has spent the past 16 years as a trusted HR advisor and coach both inside and outside of large corporations. She has successfully consulted with many Fortune 100 C-suite leadership teams in all areas of human resources including talent assessment and development, strategic workforce planning, staffing, compensation and employee relations.

Andria is the founder of C3-Corso Coaching & Consulting, an executive coaching and strategic human resources consulting firm that is dedicated to enhancing and advancing employees' careers and helping organizations and employees reach their highest potential. C3 currently offers individual and group coaching and workshops to HR teams on the concepts written about in *From Gatekeeper to Trusted Advisor: Success Strategies for Today's HR Professional.* The coaching and workshops have successfully propelled numerous HR teams to trusted advisor status and enabled them to consistently provide outstanding high-level support to their organizations.

In 2009, Andria was awarded *Training Magazine's* Top Young Trainer of the Year award for her outstanding HR leadership at Lockheed Martin Corporation, specifically for her leadership of their talent management programs, her strategic thinking capabilities and her exceptional mentoring and coaching skills.

Andria is widely recognized for her engaging style, her ability to quickly bring clarity to complex issues that face executive leaders, and her ability to effectively align HR strategy with business strategy. She is sought after for her coaching, advice and counsel in these areas and for her ability to consistently deliver high-impact results. She currently resides in Rockville, Maryland. *From Gatekeeper to Trusted Advisor: Success Strategies for Today's HR Professional* is her first book.

BRING ANDRIA
TO YOUR COMPANY!

Andria Corso is available for individual and group coaching, for speaking engagements and Bridge Principle training to help you and your HR Team reach trusted advisor status. Implement the Bridge Principles with your HR team by contacting Andria today. She will work with you to design a custom program that specifically fits the needs of you or your HR team.

Also, please visit her website for a variety of free resources:
www.andriacorso.com

And, don't forget to visit From Gatekeeper to Trusted Advisor's Readers Only Page to access all the templates, tip sheets, checklists and forms shared in this book:
www.trustedadvisorreaderspage.com

Andria Corso Contact Information:

Mail:
C3 – Corso Coaching & Consulting
P.O. Box 2472
Rockville, MD 20847

Phone:
240-558-3959

Email:
andria@andriacorso.com

Website:
www.andriacorso.com

Breinigsville, PA USA
25 October 2010
248010BV00001B/2/P